Wolves

of the Rocky Mountains

D1534091

Dick Dekker

Wolves of the Rocky Mountains

ISBN 0-88839-416-0
First published in 1994 as *Wolf Story*.
Enlarged and Updated.
Copyright © 1997 Dick Dekker

Cataloging in Publication Data
Dekker, Dick, 1933
  Wolves of the Rocky Mountains
  Includes bibliographical references and index.
  Previous ed. has title: Wolf story.

ISBN 0-88839-416-0

  1. Wolves—Alberta—Jasper National Park. 2. Wolves—Control.
  I. Title II. Title: Wolf story.
QL737.C22D435 1997   599.773'097123'32   C 97-910215-4

Editing, graphic design and line drawings by the author.
Front Cover Photo: Hank Wong

Published simultaneously in Canada and the United States by

HANCOCK HOUSE PUBLISHERS LTD.
19313 Zero Avenue, Surrey, BC V4P 1M7
(604) 538-1114   Fax (604) 538-2262

HANCOCK HOUSE PUBLISHERS
1431 Harrison Avenue, Blaine, WA 98230-5005
(604) 538-1114   Fax (604) 538-2262

TABLE OF CONTENTS

FROM JASPER TO YELLOWSTONE

Dick Dekker's *Wolves of the Rocky Mountains* chronicles not only his 33 years of wolf watching in the wilds of Alberta's Jasper National Park, but it also is an unbiased insight into the science and politics of ever-controversial wolf management. Dick's balanced perspective comes from his many years of observation, a directorship in the Canadian Wolf Defenders, participation in scientific wolf conferences, and from publishing his own wolf information. In this most recent book, he has woven a comprehensive story that needs to be told. It is the story of wolves in the Canadian wilderness, of their survival during the lean years prior to the 1970s, and of their ultimate triumph as the source population for the dramatic reintroductions to Yellowstone.

The recent transplants of wolves from Alberta and British Columbia to Yellowstone National Park and central Idaho were as controversial as the animals themselves and a story in itself, like no other. When the United States Fish and Wildlife Service first asked Alberta for wolves in August 1994, Dick and I thought it would be a win-win situation. Wolves would be returned to habitats without a wolf howl for nearly 100 years, thousands of Americans would be able to enjoy their presence, and Canadians could participate in a positive way. To a certain extent, all of this happened, but not without tremendous controversy, court decisions and ferocious battles between governments, environmental and wilderness organizations, landowners and wolf lovers. This book details the background of the ancient wolf-human relationship and explains why this transplant was so contentious.

Dick's fascination with wildlife centers on predators. For much of the past 40 years and at his own expense, he has watched peregrine falcons, red foxes, wolves and other predators do what comes naturally. But, he has done more than that. He has written of his adventures with the color and understanding that come with first-hand experience.

Wolves have become one of the most studied of earth's creatures. We now know that wolf predation is highly complex and can be an important limitation to prey populations. As wolves are returned to more and more of their original North American range, a good understanding of their role and effect is required. With more knowledge, the dilemma of wildlife managers—how to provide abundant hoofed mammals and, at the same time, maintain healthy populations of wolves—will be better appreciated. Reestablished wolves in Yellowstone and other former habitats of the American West will undoubtedly bring some problems for cattlemen, and perhaps in time reduced big game for hunters. Nevertheless, surely there is some room here for one of the world's most tenacious and interesting large carnivores. The general public needs to know the full story of wolves and wolf management, and this book is a great step in that direction.

John R. Gunson
Wildlife Management Biologist (Large Carnivores)
Alberta Environmental Protection

VIEW FROM
THE HOWLING HILL

On either side of the valley, steep mountains rise into the clear autumn sky. Their lower slopes are wrapped in a mantle of evergreen, contrasting darkly with the brilliance of golden poplars that line the blue river meandering over the valley bottom.

On a semi-open island formed by the braided stream, graze two dozen elk, all females. Nearby struts a stag with enormous antlers, six points on each beam, polished to gleaming daggers. His regal posture demands attention and his body colors are designed for visual impact; the yellow-tan on back and rump catches the sunlight, while the blackish-brown on belly and legs underscores his massive bulk. From time to time, the stag raises his maned head and bugles a high-pitched challenge to his rivals hidden in the forest.

A little separate from the herd, there are four elk cows accompanied by calves, about two-thirds the size of their mothers. Unlike the other elk on the island, the four are not nibbling on the vegetation but stand in an alert pose, head raised, looking into the same direction. Suddenly, one of the cows startles and trots off, followed by the other three and their calves. The herd stops grazing. All heads are now turned. A few seconds later, the animals run away. They plunge through the river channel and head for the woods on the other side.

What is the cause of their fear? Look to the right! Three black wolves are streaking over the island. They splash through the water and overtake the last of the herd. One of the cows dodges and turns to make a stand in the shallow river. When a wolf lunges at her rump, she kicks with her hind legs and flees, crossing and recrossing the channel until she finds a deep spot where the water foams with turbulence and reaches to her belly.

On one side, the rapids are flanked by a steep cliff. On the open shore opposite, the three wolves have come to a halt, pacing back and forth. One of them enters the river and tries to swim to the elk, but she wades out of reach against the strong current. Unable to get close to his prey, the wolf maintains a hold on a shallow spot or submerged boulder. Only his black head is visible in the choppy water. He stays there for almost fifteen minutes.

At intervals, one of the wolves on the bank emits a muffled bark. Is he telling his pack mates to press on? Or has he become aware of the person sitting on a nearby hillside, watching through binoculars? Presently, the wolves give up the siege and walk back to the main island where they meet up with six other wolves. One of them is a large tan-colored animal, the other five are romping pups.

Partly hidden from view by a screen of willow bushes, the family members mingle, tails wagging, until one of the black wolves leads the pack away. They cross the river channel in single file, each animal holding its tail straight up out of the current. The pups are almost submerged in the deepest water. Two black wolves bring up the rear. Without pausing on the other side, the pack files into the forest, heading into the same direction as the elk have gone.

The cow elk that stood off her attackers stays in the river for another twenty minutes, until she walks stiffly and hesitantly to the shore. All the while, the big stag, ignored and bypassed by the wolves, has remained on the island. As if to vent his frustration and rage, he is thrashing a willow bush with savage swipes of his antlers.

The above incident took place one October morning in 1988 along the Athabasca River in Jasper National Park, Alberta, while I watched from the "howling hill", not far from the main Yellowhead highway that transects the park. The chance of seeing wolves in Jasper, even along the roads, is available to any lucky

visitor. In fact, many nature lovers from around the world come to the park especially for such a chance. But that opportunity was not always there.

When I first came to Canada, in 1959, there were plenty of elk in Jasper, but large carnivores were not wanted. The first coyote I ever saw was shot by park wardens, right before my eyes, while I was observing it from the roadside. By the mid 1950s, wolves had been practically exterminated in all of western Alberta. Until 1966, the placing of poison baits remained a routine form of predator control practised each winter in provincial forests north of the national park, and in some years even inside the park. And nobody seemed to care! In those days, attitudes toward predators were still in the dark ages. Hatred and fear of wolves were rampant among country folk and even professional biologists. In 1964, a year of record cold and snowfall, a provincial wildlife manager was quoted in the *Edmonton Journal* as follows: "Anyone who faces a wolf pack this winter takes his life in his hands!"

Today, the situation has changed very much indeed. After centuries of persecution, the wolf has become one of the most beloved wild animals in North America. Their reintroduction into the western United States, particularly Yellowstone National Park, aroused the imagination of a wide spectrum of people. Books about wolves, videos and art prints sell to an ever-widening circle of patrons. In England, France, Germany, Sweden, as well as in North America, there are numerous organizations dedicated to the study and protection of wolves. Canadians are envied for living in a part of the world where wolves and wilderness still exist in abundance. With that privilege comes a responsibility to manage our wolves as a natural treasure that is appreciated by growing masses of people in and outside Canada.

The wolf's changing image, from the feared and hated killer of the past to the wild variety of "man's best friend", did not happen overnight. It is the end product of decades of controversy and heated debate between wolf defenders and wolf killers. Wolf predation on livestock and wild game has been one of the hottest wildlife issues in recent times and all signs indicate that it will continue to be for years to come.

This book aims to portray the wolf in a sympathetic yet realistic perspective, inspired by a lifetime of observing predatory animals in the field. It includes an historical overview of mankind's war on wolves that began nearly four centuries ago, soon after the first Europeans settled in the United States and Canada. Much of the factual information on the wolf as a predator is based on the growing body of scientific literature available today. The wolf has become the most studied large carnivore, perhaps even the most studied wild animal species of all time. Some of the chapters focus on the changing theories of wildlife managers and on the discoveries made by field researchers. Other chapters, on the wolf's family life, ecology, and interaction with prey species, are largely based on personal experience in Jasper National Park. All anecdotes of wolf behavior described in these pages are exactly as observed in the wild.

Unattached to government departments or institutes of higher education, I have been free from the constraints that usually force professional wildlife researchers to do their field work over the short term. To prove or disprove a postulated hypothesis, biologists seek hard data, involving the capture and manipulation of their subjects. During my observations I tried to prevent undue disturbance, allowing wolves and their prey species to teach me in their own subtle way, over the long term. Nevertheless, much of what I learned about the interaction of carnivores and ungulates is owed to the publications of the professionals, particularly those named in these chapters and in the reference section. Comments attributed to scientists quoted in this book were taken from articles and interviews that appeared in *WolfNews* (published by Canadian Wolf Defenders and financially supported by World Wildlife Fund Canada) of which

I was editor during its ten years of publication. Biologists John Gunson, François Messier and Ann Lukey kindly reviewed the manuscript and made helpful comments. However, the opinions expressed on these pages and the accuracy of statements attributed to others remain the responsibility of the author.

My long fascination with wolves is intertwined with a quest for wilderness, for original landscapes where plant and animal associations are still complete and not greatly disrupted by humans. The search for wolves has taken me to the Yukon, to Alaska and the precambrian shield country of northern Saskatchewan, where my wife and I canoed more than two thousand miles on remote rivers and lakes. In the Rocky Mountains, I back-packed for hundreds of days along the hiking trails of Jasper, often in solitude, sleeping in a pup tent on the edge of wolf rendezvous sites. During winter, I spent long evenings in a backcountry cabin or tent, contemplating the universe in a silent monologue, grateful for the glow of a candle and the radiance of a woodstove. The breaking of dawn and the gentle gathering of dusk were the greatest shows on earth. During the brief daylight hours, observations of animals or their tracks provided entertainment and discovery.

Over the years, several wolf packs have learned to tolerate and even ignore me, the greatest compliment a wild animal can bestow on a human. Other than the thrill of just observing them, I have wanted nothing from these wolves. Carrying no camera, I refrained from approaching them and felt guilty of trespass when I stumbled onto their lair or involuntarily disrupted their business. The one indiscretion I allowed myself was to howl like a wolf from a lookout-hill, each morning and evening, in the hope of getting an answer from my wild brothers. The resident pack soon recognized the weird wail and observed me from a distance, probably with a grin of amusement on their faces. They certainly showed no fear. They were the rulers in their game-rich territory, with roots going back over the millennia, and I was but a stranger in paradise.

This book is dedicated to all those who fight for the preservation of parks, wilderness and wolves, but especially to members and supporters of the former Canadian Wolf Defenders. The society was founded in 1968 by Alberta artist Robert Guest and disbanded in 1992 after wolf defenders everywhere had achieved a major victory. In the opinion of CWD's long-term president Arne Jonasson, the need for a group that limited itself to the defense of wolves had greatly diminished. "The big bad wolf is no more. The animal is now a much loved and appreciated member of the Canadian fauna."

I am thankful to Jasper wardens for logistical support in the field under a Volunteer Wildlife Researcher contract initiated in 1987. Senior warden Wes Bradford has been generous with information which contributed greatly to this story of the wolves of Jasper. Alberta carnivore manager John Gunson provided research data on the Brazeau wolf pack, as well as stimulating discussion and relevant literature on wolf studies from across the continent. Frequent companions in the field were Peter DeMulder and Brian Genereux, who shared the joys and hazards of winter camping, when Orion glittered in the cold of night, or when gale-force Chinooks raised clouds of dust from the dry river bed and obscured the view from the howling hill.

Part I

WATCHER IN THE WILDERNESS

A passion for observing,
an obsession for truths and origins,
leads us back to wolves and wilderness,
where it all begins.

Chapter 1

CRY OF THE WILD

Dusk is settling over Rocky Mountain wilderness. The black spires of spruce, like the steeples of churches, point up at a flawless sky. While the golden afterglow of sundown dims over distant hills, a full moon rises, its brightening globe reflected in a mirror of smooth water.

We sit on the shore by a dying fire, red embers crackling, a small intimate sound magnified by the silence around us. Soon the dusk will deepen and we prepare ourselves mentally to get up, ready for sleep under canvas. But the languid setting holds us in its magic. Are we hoping for a signal to break the spell?

Far away, on the edge of hearing, echoes a cry, falling away again before we are fully aware of it. Listen! Mouth half open, barely breathing, we wait until the call comes again. It is a high-pitched wail, rising in volume and held at its loudest level for a few moments, until it breaks into a rich baritone that ebbs away in melancholy modulations. Silence closes in once more, but we dare not move for a long time, until a shiver makes us hunch our shoulders. Is it the cold creeping up? Or the stirring of atavistic memories from an ancient past when our primitive ancestors slept under the stars and were often serenaded by brother wolf, setting out on his night-time hunt.

Why does this blood-stained predator have such a sweet, beautiful voice? Why does our own species have the ability to create music that melts the heart, yet humans are capable of the most despicable cruelty and violence, against our own kind and against other creatures. It is a paradox that continues to baffle the deepest of intellects.

To best appreciate the bewitching charm of a wolf's howl, we should hear the animal by itself, so that we can follow the full range of its voice from its eerie rising to the very last note, uninterrupted by the calls of other wolves. When several animals howl at the same time, individual voices are submerged, but a group howl can have its own special impact. The members of a pack take care not to sing on exactly the same tone as their mates, shifting a note or so to avoid overlap. The combined effect is meant to impress. A chorus howl transfers upon the listener an idea of the size and strength of the pack. The more wolves in the group, the more awesome their chorus, echoing against a backdrop of forest or mountain as a celebration of tribal power, like the drums of an Indian war party.

The sweetness and musical timbre of wolf song are perhaps at their most alluring during the mating season, when an amorous pair goes courting and serenades each other under a clear sky on a winter's night. A million stars blaze above, not a breath of wind sighs in the spruces. The temperature is far below freezing. Lying in our tent, in warm sleeping bags, we turn on our back and listen with total concentration.

There is one wolf in the hills behind our camp, the other on the flats by the river. They call alternately, over and over, each time in exactly the same melodious phrase, but one animal has a higher voice than the other. At first they are far off, but gradually they move closer, until their calls fade away again into the distance. The high-pitched howl remains audible for a long time, pure and innocent as the cry of a child.

What was their message to each other? We can only guess. Like any dog, wolves are social creatures and they lead highly emotional lives that quicken to a pace we cannot understand. When they are amorous or lonely, they express their longing to the sky and to the stars. It is a lucky person who hears the song of wolves in the sterile silence of winter, a call of the wild that resonates in our trembling heart.

There was a time when the howling of wolves was greatly dreaded by man the shepherd, who turned over in his sleep uneasily and shuddered at the prospect of a slaughtered flock in the morning. But we, who can enjoy the best of both worlds, the amenities of towns and cities as well as the solitude of a day or two in the wilds on our own terms, we have no such worries. Modern-day wilderness travelers can appreciate the beguiling howl of wolves for its own sake.

Why and when do wolves howl? What exactly is its purpose? These questions have been posed repeatedly by scientists, some of whom have done field work to determine at which times of day and in which season wolves are most vocal. But by and large, the obvious reasons why wolves howl are hard to translate into scientifically valid meaning.

Wolves definitely do not howl to entertain humans, neither to strike fear into their prey. They howl to contact other wolves, for mutual benefit, to exchange information on whereabouts, status and intentions. When a pack is traveling or hunting, howling serves as a means of keeping in touch with straying members of the group. Lone wolves may howl to find friendly strangers or to avoid hostile encounters. Territorial packs are ever-ready to return the calls of interlopers as a warning to stay away and avoid bloodshed.

Does this mean that wolves have the ability to distinguish one howl from the other? Or that they can recognize individuals at a distance by their howls? They probably can. Even people can learn to tell the difference between some howls. A pup's soprano is a far cry from the gruff moan of an old lobo. Some wolves have a specially deep or squeaky voice, others may vary their call, sounding either high or low on different occasions. High-pitched, richly modulated howls of subordinate pack members are probably more inviting and less threatening to other wolves than the deep sustained baritone of some dominant animals. However, it remains to be proven whether deepness of voice has much to do with size, status or age.

The howl of a wolf that is disturbed by our presence may not sound very pleasant at all. It is often brief and interrupted with barking. Thus, the tone of a wolf's call is affected by its state of mind. Some people believe that wolves can convey all sorts of information by their howls, such as whether they are lonely, hungry or hunting, or in need of help in overcoming large prey or ambushing a herd. But how can we be sure?

It is very difficult and often misleading to interpret the intentions of a wolf by its howl or even its actions. With limited senses and muddled instincts, we are but intruders into the realm of animals. After a lifetime of watching in the field, with luck and patience, we may learn some new insight and contribute a little to our collective understanding of the species. The wolf is a wild animal of great individual resources, capable of making a living in the wilderness on its own. Yet, like humans, it is a social creature, tied down to an inherited code of behavior imprinted in its genes by its ancestors and reinforced continually by its contemporaries. To communicate with its fellows, a wolf has several direct and indirect ways of expressing itself, even over the long distance. Howling is just one of them and it happens to be very pleasing to us.

The interesting fact that wolves will actually answer human imitations of their howls was probably well-known to people who lived close to the land in the past. For example, the Russian novelist Tolstoy mentions it in his 1862 classic *The Cossacks*. But the relatively recent discovery of the willingness of wolves to howl back at human imitators, and its implications for research, was made in 1959 in Algonquin Provincial Park, Ontario. At that time, the late Douglas Pimlott, the dean of Canadian wolf biologists, had just begun his pioneering study in the park's 7,500 square kilometers (2,880 square miles) of lake-studded forests. The region contained large numbers of deer, moose and beaver, and the wolf population was believed to be the densest anywhere, around one wolf per 25 km² (10 miles²). The total number of packs in Algonquin was later found to be around thirty.

During winter, it was fairly easy for Pimlott to find wolves on frozen lakes or in snow-covered woods where they were plainly visible from a small aircraft. By following tracks in the snow, he and his students could collect the remains of kills to determine the wolves' feeding habits. But the researchers felt seriously handicapped during summer. How to locate and study the wolves in the thick forest? At that time, the invention and wide application of radio-collars had to wait another ten years.

At the suggestion of a colleague, Pimlott had a recording made of the howls of captive wolves held in enclosures at his Wildlife Research Station. On the night of August 5, 1959, somewhere along a road in the park's interior, the recording was broadcast through a loudspeaker mounted on a vehicle. Replies were received from wild wolves after the first try! It was an historic breakthrough in the field study of the species. Before that summer was over, the researchers had located the home-sites of two wolf packs and contacted several others. It was not even necessary to use the technical equipment; the wolves appeared to be just as ready to answer reasonably accurate imitations of howling by people.

With the wolf study going on in Algonquin, some tourists became curious. They had heard or seen the researchers howling and wanted to know more about the subject. The naturalists at the park's interpretive center were often asked questions about wolves, until someone got the bright idea of inviting the public to come along on a howl.

The event was to take place on August 17, 1963. Notices had been placed at the park's information centers and in all campgrounds, but no-one seriously imagined that many people would turn out. When a few of the staff casually went down to the appointed meeting place, they found a traffic jam of 180 vehicles and over 600 people! Somehow, the jumble was sorted out and history's first public wolf howl got underway. Despite the fact that only a faint reply from one animal was received, the event was an overwhelming success and removed all doubts about the level of public interest in wolves.

Since then, interpretive staff at Algonquin Park have fine-tuned their methods in organizing a successful wolf howl program. The first step in holding an event is to locate the home-site of a pack of wolves. Teams of howlers go out on several nights during the previous week and cover the park's approximately 80 km (50 miles) of highways and secondary roads. If they get a response from a pack with pups in a suitable location, notices go up at the information centers. Other preparations include the planning of the route and the logistics of up to 16 staff members in half a dozen radio-equipped vehicles.

As described in the pamphlet *Wolf Howling in Algonquin*, on the evening of the appointed date the public is directed to park at the Outdoor Center which holds about 370 vehicles. Often the lot fills up entirely and up to a thousand people have been turned away at one time! A typical turn-out is about 250 cars which, when moving out onto the road, stretch for about 10 km (6 miles). After the cars park, they are much closer together than when on the move, but still there are so many that no-one can see the entire caravan or know when the arrivals finally stop. People wait quietly beside their vehicle with the lights off, as they had been asked to do before departure during the instruction lecture in the Outdoor Center. The degree of cooperation is always perfect. Before long, everyone is silent and looking forward to the moment when the naturalists make their first attempt to call up the wolves.

When a pack responds with a wild clamor in the darkness of

the woods, a chill runs down many a spine and deep emotions are aroused in the crowd. In the words of park naturalist Dan Strickland, for some it is the re-awakening of a longing for the wild freedom of remote ancestors, or the mystery of an animal that we all know exists but few ever see. It may be the thrill of direct communication with a legendary outlaw, including a tinge of fear carried over from childhood tales. Whatever the reason, the impact of the event is profound. A little while after the pack stops howling and silence returns, everyone starts talking excitedly. When the crowd at last heads back to campground or lodge, people carry with them a fond memory of wolf music under a star-studded sky.

The program has been expanded to four excursions per year, usually during August. In 1995 each event involved over 600 vehicles with up to 2,700 passengers! About 80 percent of attempts at calling up wolves were successful. The popularity of Algonquin is ever increasing with hundreds of inquiries from all over the world each year.

Public howling excursions have also been organized in other Canadian Parks, such as Riding Mountain in Manitoba and Prince Albert in Saskatchewan, but rarely in Banff or Jasper, where backroads are few and rough, while the main valley is noisy with transport trucks and trains day or night. Moreover, during spring and summer wolves seldom remain near the roads and disappear to hidden home-sites to raise their pups. Yet, a few startled tourists have seen wolves walking right through their campground. Other campers, during a still night, heard the cry of the wild drift down from the mountains, like a dream come true.

Chapter 2

FEAR OF FANGS

Desperate to get away from its pursuers, the deer enters and disappears into a small waterhole of the frozen Snake Indian River in Jasper National Park. Seconds later, the forerunners of the wolf pack emerge from the wooded shore. Following the trail of the deer, they bound over the snow-covered ice and come to an abrupt stop at the hole. One after the other, eight more wolves arrive, all of them black or smoke-gray. They mill about and gingerly step down to the edge of the water. One of them runs down-river to another waterhole, as if expecting the deer to emerge there. Others lope in a wide half-circle over the river, nose to the snow, searching for fresh scent. They look deadly serious, gripped with hunting fever, keen to find their prey. A few minutes later, the leaders of the pack turn back into the woods, followed by their companions. Soon all are gone from view.

Twice within the next hour or so, the wolves return to the river. Each time, some of them reinvestigate the waterhole and again run in a wide semi-circle over the ice. By the time the pack retreats into the woods for the third time, the brief winter's day is drawing to a close. Have the wild hunters finally given up on finding the deer...?

Watching through binoculars from a nearby hillside, overlooking the scene of action, my curiosity is peaked. Is the deer still in the water hole? Eager to investigate before darkness sets in, I descend the hill and head out briskly across the river that has expanded well beyond its summertime bed. Extreme cold earlier in the winter froze the river to the bottom, forcing the running water upward through cracks in the thick ice. The overflow has repeatedly inundated the banks, forming sheets of ice that extend far into shoreline woods.

Over the main channel, the ice has caved in to form a shallow gully, and a portion has opened up. The hole is no bigger than 6 by 3 meters (20 by 10 feet). The snow at the edge is packed with wolf tracks. But there is no sign of the deer. On the downstream side of the hole, the sloping ice has broken away and leaves an air space over the swiftly flowing water, like a cave. Is the deer hiding in shallows under the overhanging ice? Or has it been swept away to its death? I shall never know....

Just after I turn to leave, nearby in the woods two shadowy animals turn and run away, vanishing between the trunks of trees encased in the ice. The wolves! They must have heard my footsteps and came to investigate! What if they had mistaken me for an easy prey? The image of the big pack is still vivid on my mind: ten intense predators, eager to make a kill.

In the woods, a wolf begins to howl and bark. Is it a warning or a threat? Breaking out in perspiration, I force myself to slow down, to stop hurrying and pretend to be confident, at ease. Suddenly I halt with a jolt of paralysing fear. Standing in the snow ahead, on the edge of the woods, are four black silhouettes, like wolves watching. My eyes, that have poor night-vision, try to focus in the deepening dusk. Nervously, I grope for the binoculars. A quick glance reveals that the objects are tree trunks protruding from the ice.

It is a relief to reach the shore on the other side of the river and to climb onto the open bank, safely on the way to the warm cabin. Was my fear justified? Obviously it was not. But was it understandable? That remains for each of us to experience and feel.

Can wolves pose a direct threat to human beings? Have they ever attacked people? It is an old question, loaded with superstition, clouded by atavistic fears. Fear easily leads to hate and the urge to destroy. Some modern-day wilderness travellers still have an emotional need for the security of a gun as protection against wild animals. During summer, the main worry is bears. But wolves...? Numerous authorities have stated emphatically that the wild dogs are not dangerous to people at all. There are no reliable records, they say, that wolves have ever killed a human being, at least not in North America. Even in Canada's northern-most wilderness, where wolves encounter very few human beings, the species seems to know instinctively that we are better left alone, that we are a superior creature to be shunned or tolerated at a safe distance.

What about the old days? In the eighteenth century, when the first Europeans travelled across the western plains, wolves were apparently not averse to eating human corpses. During winter, it was the custom among natives to place their deceased, wrapped in skins, on scaffolds in trees out of reach of scavengers. When the ground was unfrozen, Indians as well as whites buried their dead and covered the graves with heavy stones. However, the diaries of the first European scouts do not indicate that wolves were considered dangerous to living people.

Biologist Douglas Pimlott explained the predator's respect for humans on the basis of body language. Wolves have the instinctive ability to recognize aggression or fear, which are evidenced in subtle ways by our expressions and actions. The way we walk may look like hunting behavior to wolves. We move deliberately as many predators do. We stalk quietly through the woods and stride confidently across the plains, just like a wolf traveling over his range and hunting for food.

According to Pimlott, our activity patterns may indicate to wolves that we are fellow hunters, not prey. Be that as it may, the question remains why wolves do not show the same respect for the most powerful predator of all, the bear. There are many reports of wolves harassing and even killing bears, blacks as well as grizzlies.

The real reason why wolves treat humans differently than any other creature may be found in the fact that North American natives and whites have always had the power to kill at a distance with bullets or arrows. Wolves, by virtue of their intelligence and learning ability, must have recognized man's magical powers long ago and the species has passed on its distrust to their offspring, indirectly or directly. When encountering the tracks or scent of humans, the reaction of parent wolves may teach their pups instinctively that this particular species is not one to be hunted, rather to be ignored or even feared.

In contrast to North America, there is no doubt that wolves have attacked and killed people in Europe, especially in southern countries where pockets of cultivation reach deep into rugged mountains. Old World peasants were not hunters but eked out a living by working the fields and herding livestock.

A notorious and well-documented case of wolves killing people occurred in France between 1764 and 1767 when the "Beast of Gévaudan" wounded over one hundred people of which 64 died, most of them children. The rampage ended after two animals were killed, both very large and weighing up to 58 kg (127 lbs), much heavier than the largest known records for southern European wolves. The suspicion is therefore justified that these man-hunters were not pure wolves but dog/wolf hybrids. There is no question that domestic dogs can be aggressive toward humans. Renegades among "man's best friend" bite and sometimes kill thousands of children and adults each year.

The classical tale of wolves devouring people is that of the

Russian nobleman in his horse-drawn troika, pursued and pulled down by a horde of rabid, slavering savages, red tongues lolling over gleaming fangs. In the absence of reliable accounts, such stories should be relegated to folklore, although it is very well possible that wolves would follow a horse-drawn sled, because of ease of travel in times of deep snow or simply out of curiosity.

Another probable reason why wolves might have attacked people in the Old Country is rabies. Animals affected by the dreaded disease lose their normal inhibitions and may bite any creature they encounter, human or animal. The risk of being bitten by a rabid wolf or dog was a grim fact of life in medieval Europe, and perhaps even today in some parts of the world.

Yet, despite the above, the question of whether wolves have ever attacked people in North America in recent times should not be dismissed too glibly. In fact, there are at least half a dozen cases on record that throw some doubt on the currently popular belief in the wolf's absolute innocence. One of the most notable incidents is supported by sworn statements given by the people involved and described in *The Journal of Mammalogy*.

It happened to Mike Dusiak, a railway section foreman who was driving his speeder at night along the main line west of Chapleau, Ontario, in the winter of 1942. He was expecting to meet a train and was moving quite slowly, so as to allow him to get off the rails in time. Suddenly something hit him, grabbed him by the left arm and pulled him and the speeder off the track. Dusiak thought at first he had been hit by a train, but when he quickly got up out of the snow, he saw a wolf coming toward him. Just in time, he got hold of an axe and defended himself vigorously, hitting the wolf on the head or body. "Growling and gnashing its teeth" it kept up the attack for about twenty minutes until a train came by. Its crew saw Dusiak's plight, stopped the locomotive and came running with picks and other tools, eventually killing the wolf. The conservation officer who examined the carcass stated that the wolf had been in apparent normal condition. It was, however, not tested for rabies, but its behavior suggested that it may have been a victim of the disease.

Also described in *The Journal of Mammalogy* are two accounts of wolves interacting with scientists in Canada's north. The first case took place on June 29, 1977, on remote Ellesmere Island, where wolves even today do not exhibit any fear of humans. On the open tundra, a pack of six white wolves approached two paleontologists who tried to hold the animals off by yelling and throwing clods of earth. The pack halted a few meters away. The tense situation was described in these words: "One of the wolves then took the lead and, looking Mary Dawson directly in the face, walked steadily forward, ignoring our poorly aimed clods. Its ears were erect and its mouth closed or just ajar. When approximately 1.5 meters (5 feet) away, the wolf leapt toward Dawson's head...who leaned back and uttered a small cry...The wolf grazed her cheek, leaving it wet with saliva, then dropped to the ground, turned and, with a few backward glances, retreated."

All six wolves eventually moved away. The motivation for their strange behavior was probably curiosity. They did not know what kind of creature they had encountered and wanted to test its mettle. The steadfastness of the scientists, their refusal to run away like the wolves' usual prey, may have inhibited a full-scale attack.

In the second case, which happened in June of 1984 near Churchill, in the far north of Manitoba, a party of three zoologists was approached silently by at least three wolves. The men were walking through the woods and had just stopped in a small open area covered with lichens. They had taken their packs off and were talking together when they heard a twig snap behind them. Turning, they saw a wolf about 9 meters (30 feet) away running directly toward them. The frightful experience was recorded as follows: "Scott responded by stamping his feet and yelling harshly. Wolf A attempted to stop and turn around at the same time, lost its balance and crashed into a shrub in the clearing, 5-6 meters (15-18 feet) away from Bentley. Meanwhile, Scott attempted to remove a bear-horn (similar to a fog horn or boat horn, used to startle polar bears) from his pack. Scott observed wolf A retreat past a large tree, while wolf B was advancing from the opposite side of the same tree, within 8 meters (25 feet) of us. Wolf B lunged toward Scott in two-meter bounds, ears up, tail straight out and its eyes locked onto his. After wolf B's second lunge, Scott sounded the bear-horn at arm's length, when the wolf was within two meters of him. Wolf B responded by blinking its eyes, twitching its ears, and completing its third lunge in a slight divergence off-course. It landed beside Scott, less than one meter away. Wolf B immediately trotted into the clearing, pausing at three meters distant."

All three scientists quickly climbed trees and watched the wolves coming and going through the open area at intervals for four hours. After the animals had not shown up for some time, the men finally retreated to their vehicle, a short distance away. Along the way, they stumbled on a wolf den. Nearby they noticed many scats and tracks, including those of pups.

Commenting on the above incidents, David Mech, North America's foremost wolf biologist, believes that if the wolves had actually been serious about attacking the scientists, the result would no doubt have been instant and deadly. The behavior exhibited by the animals seems to represent either threats, defensive reactions or some other non-predatory interactions.

Another quite recent incident of a wolf attacking a person appears to have been a case of mistaken identity. It happened in 1982 on a wintry day in the woods of Minnesota to 19-year-old Ron Poyrier, who was hunting in a dense pocket of trees when he was suddenly knocked down by a wolf. The boy rolled on the ground with the animal and grabbed it by the throat to hold it away. It kicked and clawed him but did not bite. The boy was still holding his rifle and after he managed to fire a shot, the wolf disappeared at once. At the time, Poyrier was wearing hunting clothes laced with buck scent. A likely explanation for the attack is that the wolf may have been chasing a deer and confused the boy with its regular prey.

There are several cases on record when wolves pursued dogs that ran back to their owners. In one incident, again in Minnesota, the wolf was so intent on grabbing the dog that it actually ripped the shirt of the man who held his frightened pet in his arms. For one terrifying moment, logger Sanford Sandberg looked right into the gaping mouth of the wolf before it dropped down and ran off into the bush.

In rural districts of Canada's western provinces, from Manitoba to British Columbia and north to Yukon, local newspapers quite often carry accounts of wolves entering people's yards at night to kill and devour dogs. In a few cases, when people tried to intervene, alerted by their pet's barking, the wolf reportedly lunged at the person, perhaps in its confusion to get away. Such incidents are particulary disturbing if there are children involved.

On April 28, 1987, three girls of between eight and twelve years old were walking home after school on Sturgeon Point Road, near Vanderhoof, British Columbia. Their German shepherd was running ahead. Suddenly, three wolves jumped out of the bushes at the dog, injuring its ear before it escaped through a barbed wire fence. One of the wolves came within a few meters of the girls before it too ran off through the fence and appeared to wound itself. To reassure local residents, the newspaper reporting on the incident included a brief statement by the local conservation officer that there was no evidence that the wolves meant to harm the girls. Poison baits had been placed in the area to destroy the wolves.

The above illustrates that wild wolves are by no means always deterred by the proximity of humans. A dangerous situation may develop if wolves frequent garbage dumps and get used to seeing people who do not molest them. In the summer of 1978, in the backwoods of western Ontario, close to the boundary with Manitoba, loggers frequently saw wolves that appeared to be quite fearless. On the morning of November 1, the camp cook, an

Ojibwa woman named Elsie Wolfe, left on foot along the Suffle Lake road hoping to hitch a ride to the clinic in Red Lake, where she needed to replenish her supply of medication for her epilepsy. She never arrived. Ten days later, her remains were found by a hunter who flushed two wolves and several ravens from the spot. Although local people believe that the woman may have actually been killed by the wolves, the official version is that Elsie succumbed to her epileptic condition before her body was scavenged. A few years earlier, in the same district, a local pilot had disappeared. His aircraft was found a few days later but all that remained of the man were gnawed bones.

In a more recent case, in July of 1988, Mike Marsh was rudely awakened when a wolf pulled him out of his thick sleeping bag outside his cabin on Tibbles Lake, west of Quesnell, British Columbia. The wolf backed up a few paces when Mike yelled. When his brother came out of the cabin, both men yelled and the animal calmly loped out of sight. Wildlife officer Al Lay believed that the wolf was used to feeding at an area junk yard and that it may have confused the sleeping man with garbage. A wolf thought to be the same animal was later shot by a local rancher.

In the winter of 1992-1993, a lone wolf that had been hanging around a logging camp near Fort Nelson, British Columbia, gave two loggers the fright of their lives. "He never hesitated, he came right at me," Tony Buerge said. He had been shouting and waving his arms while his partner went up a tree. By kicking with his heavy boots, Tony managed to keep the lunging wolf at bay for seven minutes. When he threw his hardhat at the animal, it began to chew on the foam-filled earmuffs, which gave the two men a chance to run to their truck and grab a rifle.

Conditions that allow wolves to become accustomed to people, who tolerate their presence at close range, exist particularly in national and provincial parks. During the night of August 9, 1987, a lone wolf that had entered the Whitefish Campground in Algonquin Park, Ontario, bit the forearm of a 16-year-old girl. She had been sitting by a fire when the wolf, chased by two boys, ran past a group of kids and came right up to her. She shone a flashlight in its face, whereupon the wolf bit her, then let go, scratched at a tent and carried off a shoe. The wound was only superficial, but on the advice of doctors, the girl was taken to a hospital to start anti-rabies treatment. Park wardens shot the wolf later that night and sent the carcass for rabies testing. It proved negative.

Prior to the biting incident, a tame or fearless wolf had often been seen along the park's highway. During July and August, the wolf's behavior seemed oriented toward people. It ran up to human howlers at night, jumped up at car doors and bumped against people. It was even reported to have tugged at a man's collar and pulled a woman's hair. Also the previous year a fearless wolf frequented the park's roadsides.

During the mid-seventies a tame wolf called "Rosie" became quite popular, and a decade earlier, in 1963, an unusually tame wolf had been shot. It too tested non-rabid. However, none of the earlier reports involved an animal as bold as the 1987 wolf, nor did they impress human observers as a threat. The biting incident was in fact the only one reported in the park in 25 years, until there were again two cases in 1995. They involved a young lady of twenty and a boy of nine. The latter was bitten quite seriously in his side while he was walking down a trail at night. In 1996 a fearless wolf entered a campground during the night and clamped his jaws on the head of a 12-year-old boy, who was sleeping in the open. He was dragged along for several meters. Both wolves were shot and proved free of rabies. These bizarre incidents were exceptional and may in part be a consequence of the great numbers of tourists who come to Algonquin.

In Jasper, fearless wolves are very rare. In 1995 a black animal, that was often seen along the roads, closely approached a small party of people sitting around a fire. Fortunately, they did not panic and the wolf left soon after. Later, a cyclist complained that he had been chased by "a large black dog" that suddenly shot out of the forest.

Some authorities have suggested that these "tame" wolves may be former pets released by their owners. While this remains a possibility, particularly in view of the many captive wolves in private hands, the fact that some wild wolves become habituated to humans and lose their former shyness should not come as a great surprise. It is not at all unusual for other wild canids, such as foxes and coyotes, to become beggars in our parks. Coyotes can even be dangerous and unpredictable. In 1988, there were at least eight reports of coyotes biting people in Banff, Jasper and near Creston, British Columbia. In three of these incidents, the coyotes severely mauled children and attempted to drag them away into bushes, apparently treating their victims as prey.

Attacks on humans by other carnivorous species, such as bears and cougars, are quite common in Canada. Even normally docile herbivores, such as moose and bison, have chased and wounded people, albeit not to prey on them. In defense of their young or during the rutting season, elk have become the most aggressive wild animal in Jasper and Banff Parks.

By comparison, in the final analysis, wild wolves have shown unusual restraint, even during the most extreme provocation when people have invaded their dens and carried away their pups. In fact, it seems nothing short of a miracle that attacks on humans by wolves are actually so rare, a tribute to the intelligence and timid nature of this once feared predator.

Chapter 3

ROCKY MOUNTAIN RENDEZVOUS

The languid summer day draws to a close. Spruce shadows lengthen and creep out over the uneven mountain meadow. On a grassy knoll, studded with the vermilion cups of wood lily and purple clusters of wild vetch, two adult wolves are curled up asleep, some distance from each other. From time to time, one of them raises its head to look at the six puppies playing and squabbling below. Suddenly, alerted by a call, all of them race to the edge of the meadow. Between the trees, a black wolf comes into view, head held high. In its muzzle it carries a dark object, a beaver, the prize of its afternoon hunt. Its arrival is met by the puppies and the two adults in a frenzy of excitement, tails wagging vigorously. Mobbed and surrounded, the black wolf is the picture of pride, like a beaming father bringing Christmas presents to his kids.

Few scenes in nature are as heart-warming to watch as a family of wolves. Quite unlike the sullen and snarling creatures often seen in films of captive wolves, wild packs live a life of happy harmony, filled with play and loving interactions with each other. The puppies get treated princely, caressed and provided for not only by their parents, but by all adults and yearlings in a generous way that can only be described as altruistic. Wolves even bring food to wounded pack members, animals that have been crippled by accidents, bullets or traps and are unable to hunt for themselves.

The underlying characteristic of wolf society that makes a relaxed relationship between these well-armed predators possible is a finely-tuned system of order. Every pack member knows exactly who is boss, who is above it in social status, but also who is under it. This "pecking order" or dominance hierarchy is established early and confirmed during every interaction by ritualized posturing that minimizes serious outbreaks of violence.

The social system of wolf packs has been the subject of numerous studies by biologists as well as psychologists who believe that mankind can learn much about itself by observing wolves. In our dim past, tribal societies of *Homo sapiens* may have been shaped by similar forces that are still at work in *Canis lupus*. One of the basic discoveries was that wolf groups adhere to two separate orders, one for each sex. The highest ranking animals are called alpha male and alpha female. They usually produce the year's litter of young, and are in charge of most group activities, such as deciding on a home-site, departure or defense.

By studying captive packs, that allowed close and continuous observation, the Dutch wolf ethologist Ruud Derix and his colleagues learned that female wolves are more intolerant of each other than males. Alpha females show their conflict with others of their sex by frequent dominance displays, not only during courtship but also in other social interactions such as feeding and howling. By contrast, males seldom interfere with each other except during the mating period when they can be quite aggressive, for instance when a lower ranking male tries to mate with a female. The relatively high level of intolerance among the females might explain why wild wolf packs generally contain more males than females.

Wolves are believed to mate for life and only the alpha animals are allowed to breed. While this may be generally true, there are exceptions to the rule. Some alpha males refrain from copulation and then a lower-ranking or beta male breeds the alpha female. The dominant pair usually interferes at once when subordinate pack members try to mate, but pop and mom are not always around when the younger generation gets the urge! In Alaska, researchers have documented several cases where two or even three females belonging to the same pack gave birth to pups in different dens, several miles apart. Later during summer, the families were reunited and by autumn some packs ended up with more than twenty-five members! In Wolf Park, Indiana, multiple litters have also been observed, but usually only the pups of one of the females were raised successfully. In several instances, after the dominance order had been disturbed, severe fighting broke out between pregnant or nursing females, often mother and daughter, resulting in the death of one of them.

A family of wild wolves can start with just two animals of the opposite sex, but well-established packs include three or more adults that may or may not be directly related. Their offspring stays with the pack at least until they are sexually mature, at about 22 months, well after the next batch of pups is born. In their second year, some of the yearlings disperse to find a mate and raise their own family on vacant territory, or they join other packs, sometimes far away from their place of birth.

Until quite recently, it was generally believed that wolf packs are highly inbred because they actively repel strangers, but that is not always the case. Field research in Alaska, where almost 300 packs have been closely monitored with radio-telemetry, has revealed that long-range interchange of wolves is common from one end of the state to the other and well beyond its boundaries with Canada. During a recent study in Alaska's Denali National Park, where 122 wolves were radio-collared, 35 percent ended up in other packs. These findings were corroborated by genetic studies (DNA fingerprinting) that revealed links between far-flung wolf families and a fair amount of genetic diversity between members of the same groups.

An interchange of breeding stock over a wide area is beneficial to any species. But how is this allowed to happen in wolf society where individual families are strongly defensive of their home turf and drive off intruders? How can they accept a stranger in their midst? Again, this is made possible by a deeply rooted wolf-etiquette that leaves no doubt as to the newcomer's intentions. Top ranking wolves carry their tail and heads high, ears pricked up. Low status animals, during interactions with higher-ranking animals, keep their ears flat, head low, and the tail may be tucked between the legs. To prostrate themselves even further, the subordinate animal rolls over on its back, exposing its vulnerable throat and underside. It is a clear signal of submission and meant to inhibit aggressive reactions in the dominant animal. When a pack meets a lone wolf, the outcome will depend on protocol, on the proper exchange of body language. The leaders of the pack may allow the stranger to join if it is submissive. On the other hand, a strong and dominant wolf might be welcomed into a pack that has recently lost its own alpha male and happens to be in need of a leader. Similarly, a lone female might be welcomed enthusiastically by a gang of only males. However, if equals meet, for instance neighboring packs on the edge of their territories, and both parties stand their ground, hostilities are inevitable. A wolf that knowingly trespasses on occupied territory may turn tail and flee. Then the chase is on and often leads to fatal fights.

Wolf populations everywhere are subject to very high mortality rates, frequently over 30 percent per year, through the combined impact of man-made and natural causes. Even in protected areas, such as Alaska's Denali National Park, the wolf population was found to have a death rate of about 22 percent per year, and about half of these mortalities were caused by their own kind, by intra-specific aggression. The Denali study also found a high rate of pack dissolution and new formation. The boundaries of home ranges proved to be far from permanent, making the 24,000 km^2 (9,400 miles^2) park a constantly changing mosaic of about 25 pack territories.

Given its well-ordered family life, why should there be so much strife and so little stability in the wolf population as a whole? It is part of nature's plan to promote stability over the long haul. In the short term, the northern ecosystem is extremely changeable itself. A severe winter can devastate prey populations such as moose and deer. By contrast, during a series of mild winters, hoofed mammals can rebuild to far greater densities than before. They may become so numerous, in fact, that they do irreparable damage to their own winter range. To dampen prey fluctuations, there is a need for a predator with the ability to respond quickly to changing environmental conditions, for its own benefit as well as for the good of the larger ecosystem. The wolf has that adaptability. If there is plenty of food, packs raise large broods, which leads to more packs and smaller territories. On the other hand, if prey is scarce, few young survive and the pack has to hunt over a larger area to find enough to eat, which leads to more competition and more fatal encounters between the packs. When times of plenty return, wolves can quickly recover and double their population in one year. The key to this flexibility is their high breeding potential.

For an affectionate animal such as the wolf, it is little wonder that courtship continues year-round. Strong ties are maintained between the alpha pair by mutual snuffling and nose touching which looks like the equivalent of kissing in the human species. She may place her forepaws on his neck or shoulders in a tender embrace. When the mating season approaches, between January and March, the male becomes as playful as a puppy, lowering his front quarters and springing up to the female, tail wagging emphatically. He may nip her ears and try to mount her from the side or the rear. If she is not in oestrus, she may be coy, dodging his approach or sit on her tail. Only a few courtship interactions actually end up in copulation. During the fairly brief period when the female is in full heat, she solicits his attention without inhibition by lifting her tail and showing her genitals.

During the act of mating, the male becomes locked to the female by the copulatory tie, which is peculiar to the dog family. The tie is caused by swelling of distal glands in the penis and by contraction of the female's vaginal sphincter muscles. After the tie takes effect, the male dismounts and stands or lies down tail to tail with the female for up to half an hour. The event holds great fascination to other members of the pack and all run over excitedly to watch what pop and mom are doing...!

Well before she is due to give birth, about 62 days after insemination, the female will prepare a den, usually a burrow in well-drained sandy soil with one or more entrances of at least 35 cm (1 foot) wide. A large mound of soil lies in front of the main burrow that extends 2-5 meters (6-17 feet) into the ground and leads to a wider chamber where the births will take place.

Each territory contains several or even dozens of old dens and the wolves seem to know them all. If you follow the pack's trail during late winter, you will find that one of the animals, perhaps the female, makes little detours to inspect dens along the way. At some sites, there may be evidence of recent digging and you may feel delighted to have found the location of this year's den. But when you come back in early June, hoping to see the puppies, there may be no sign of activity at all. Wolves frequently change their mind and the final choice of natal den is made quite late, just before the pups are born sometime in April or May.

The usual number of young is between four and seven. They weigh about 450 grams (1 lbs) and are blind and deaf for about two weeks. Initially, the mother spends a lot of time underground, only leaving briefly for a drink from the nearest stream or pond. During the nursing period, she is supplied with food by the male.

The great day, for all wolves belonging to the pack, comes after about three weeks, when the young finally scurry outside the burrow. Standing on wobbly legs, dazed by the bright light, the most timid of the siblings soon hurry back down to the warmth and familiarity of the underground, but their innate curiosity will eventually get the better of them. Before long, all will be romping or dozing in the sun.

It is a good idea not to disturb denning wolves during April and May, but in early June it can be quite safe for a visit if you observe some basic rules. Approach the area quietly, stay away from the den itself and be content to watch from a distance. Never overstay your welcome and leave as soon as the wolves begin to bark. It is their way of telling you that your presence is disturbing them. If you persist, they may abandon the site and take the puppies away to another den. However, if you behave with due respect, the pack may end up trusting you and eventually repay you with the greatest compliment a wild animal is capable of, by tolerating and ignoring your presence.

Surprised at close range, a wolf may utter a single "woof" and run off. However, if it is really alarmed, it may not go far and bark continuously in a threatening way, much like a German shepherd. It can be quite unnerving to suddenly hear the explosive protest of a wolf behind you in the woods when you sit quietly against a tree at the edge of the denning area. It is important to retreat immediately by the same way you came, calmly and as casually as you can.

In the Rocky Mountains and boreal forests of Canada, most wolf dens are well hidden in dense growth that allows no opportunity for observation, quite unlike the northern tundra. But they are usually not far from some open or semi-open ground, such as a meadow or bog, where you can keep an eye on the den site area from a safe distance. Watching through binoculars, it is a thrill to get an intimate and detailed view, or even a glimpse, of the animals as they come and go.

During the day, the adults will be sleeping in the shade, at the base of a spruce tree, inactive until evening. When the parents are out hunting, another pack member may stay behind to baby-sit. Rarely, there is a crippled adult, unable to travel with its mates, that stays with the pups. But in many instances, the puppies are left alone, sometimes for 24 hours.

By the time the youngsters are about one-third grown, they are as cute as any young dog with a chubby babyface and oversized feet. Especially in the west, differences in pelage color make it possible to recognize some of them as individuals; coal-black with a white spot on the chest, or pale tan-gray with darker legs and tail. They are not afraid to explore their surroundings on their own, sometimes for quite a distance away from the den. It is a great thrill to have them come up to you to investigate your still form. They may even want to smell your boots! But the slightest movement on your part, perhaps to make a picture, causes them to dash off quickly. Watching wild animals is most rewarding when you leave the camera at home.

In their ceaseless play with each other, young wolves very soon establish their dominance order based on individual character traits and physical capacities. Some are aggressive and inquisitive, others passive and timid. Once they know who is boss, they relax and have fun, wrestling and grasping each other, even in rudimentary sexual postures, reinforcing the emotional attachments that will hold them together as a pack later on. They also start howling at an early age, and there is no greater delight for the watcher than to see their eager reaction to a distant howl that announces the approach of adults.

The pups halt their play and listen attentively. It takes a few moments before they respond in obvious ecstasy, raising their chubby muzzles to the sky. Their voices are high-pitched and they do a lot of yapping, much like coyotes, but some of them make a serious effort to keep up a sustained whine. A few minutes after they begin, their shrill chorus suddenly stops and they sit still in keen expectation, listening and watching. When an adult arrives, the puppies will see or hear it much earlier than you do and all of a sudden they will race away as if propelled by a cannon. They swarm around the big wolf and vie with each other to kiss or nuzzle him or her on the mouth. It is called food-begging behavior and the adult is compelled to respond.

With a cough that is audible from quite far away, it disgorges part of its stomach content, a semi-liquid mess of meat from its latest meal. It is instantly swallowed by the pups. Carrying food inside the stomach makes sense for several reasons. It facilitates transportation and the meat stays clean and out of reach of flies. The fact that it is pre-digested is an advantage for the pups. It helps them in the process of weaning, for eventually mother will stop lactating and pushes them away.

At times, the adults bring in small animals, such as rabbits or beaver, or even birds. Pieces of larger prey, such as deer or moose, are accepted by the pups with obvious delight. Leg bones remain their favorite toy long after all edible tissue has been chewed off. Stashed away in a secret corner, they will be rediscovered later and fought over with the others all over again. Tough pieces of hide and skin are torn up and worried in the same way as the young wolves will attack real prey later on, after their milk teeth have been replaced by fangs and shearing molars.

The big day arrives when the adults take their growing youngsters along for a trip to the remains of a kill not far off. At this stage, the puppies have begun to spend most of their time above ground and they are always eager for the company of adults. The return of their mom or a favorite uncle is welcomed rambunctiously and they run out at once to meet and follow them. The adults have little trouble coaxing the youngsters along on the wolf trails that radiate out from the den site. At the kill, the puppies chew and tug to their heart's content. Shoulder to shoulder, young and old gather around the table. Two of them, the alpha male and female, hold their tails up, waving like flags.

Sometime during July or August, the wolf family moves to another site that may be several miles away, where the pups stay put while the adults go out hunting. These so-called rendezvous sites are quite traditional and usually include some open terrain not far from a water source, a river or lake. The parents allow their youngsters lots of freedom to roam around, yet they seem to keep an eye on things like a good parent should. One day, six puppies approached a very steep riverbank in Jasper National Park, perhaps to get a drink, but the location was hazardous. If the pups had tried to descend the slope, they would have been in great danger of falling into the water that was swollen after heavy rains and flowing with great turbulence by the base of the slope. Just as the pups reached the top of the bank, an adult wolf emerged from the trees and called the youngsters back from the brink, so to speak.

Young wolves may occasionally run afoul of predators such as bears or even cougars that are attracted to the rendezvous site by the remains of prey or surplus meat that the wolves cache for later use. Thus, too much food carries its own risk. However, the greatest mortality cause, that sometimes strikes the entire litter, is starvation. The pups are the first to succumb if the pack has difficulty providing for its members, perhaps after one or more of the adults have been lost through accidents or other causes. By contrast, well-fed youngsters grow fast and reach over two-thirds of adult-size by autumn. When the nights become frosty and the Northwind brings the first snow, the young wolves should be fit enough to accompany their parents on major trips.

The departure of the entire pack, usually in early evening, is an event that calls for a little ceremony. It may begin with the stirring of two animals that meet each other in a friendly manner, tails wagging, one of them licking the muzzle of the other, in a submissive, food-begging ritual. Flanks touching, they trot side by side into the meadow to meet the pups. Their small yelping sounds carry in the calm of evening to the other wolves sleeping in the woods. Eager to join, they come running, and all assemble in a tight circle, pressing inwards to touch the alpha animals, tails wagging. Yipping and yapping, they raise their muzzles and howl. The high-pitched chimes of the young combine with the deep resonance of mature voices in an sustained outburst of emotion, a celebration of togetherness, a pledge of loyalty to the group, to its leaders and to each other. The pack howl stops as abruptly as it began, in a matter of minutes. One after the other, the wolves trot off, disappearing into the dusky woods.

Once they decide to move, the hunters in a wolf pack set a brisk pace and seldom look back. The youngsters easily fall behind. When they finally catch up after a kill has been made, there may not be much left but skin and bones. Chewing on the scraps, a pup may dawdle and all of a sudden find itself alone. What to do but cry and howl...? A distant response from other wolves or even a poor imitation by a person, will make the pup come running, anxious for company. If no-one answers to its anguished cries, it may remain where it is or decide to go back home.

Perhaps even more so than most mammals, a wolf has a built-in compass that guides it confidently through the wilderness. Its brain, programmed by the instinctive knowledge of millennia, develops a cognitive map of its home range based on a thousand inputs, on landmarks such as odd stones, tufts of grass, bones and antlers, or on sights, sounds and, particularly, smells. At strategic crossroads or turns of the trail, the wolves establish scent posts by depositing a few drops of urine or a scat. The purpose is two-fold; to warn or give notice of occupancy to strangers, and to supply information to pack members.

Throughout fall and winter, lone pups that have lost contact with their pack, find their way back to the main rendezvous site. Howling frequently, they wait, perhaps for several days and nights, until the pack comes by again on its rounds over its vast domain. No greater joy in the animal kingdom than a lonesome wolf pup reunited with its loving family!

Chapter 4

INNOCENT KILLERS

The seven wolves are curled up in sleep, noses warmly tucked under their bushy tail. From afar, they look like mole hills, bumps of soil sticking up out of the snow. A pair of adults is lying side by side at the base of a large spruce. Four pups of the year, almost as big as their parents, are scattered over the semi-open hilltop. From time to time, they raise their head and glance at their siblings. One of them gets up briefly and strolls over to the only remaining youngster of last year.

Like the rest of the pack, the yearling has a belly-full of meat and is in no mood for play. The pup plops down close to its big brother and goes back to sleep. Its child-like yawn carries through the still winter air to a fox in the woods below. Ears cocked, it halts for a moment, then continues its search for the source of the pungent odor that hangs between the trees. From a nearby muskeg come the sounds of ravens, cackling to each other in subdued voices as if they are sharing a secret.

The carcass of a cow moose lies where she made her last stand. Except the head and lower legs, not much is left but skin and bones. The snow around is strewn with hair and the peculiar turf-like lumps of stomach content. Soon, other scavengers, such as the fox, will carry off the bones and gnaw on the skull until not a scrap of edible tissue remains. They will also eat the red snow.

Just before nightfall, when the sleeping wolves are ready to resume travel, they may return to their kill for a brief check before going on their way. When next they pass by this area, perhaps in a week's time, the wolves will revisit the muskeg. They will recall the excitement of the hunt, how they flushed the wheezing, stiff-legged moose out of her steaming bed and chased her across bumpy, snow-covered ground until she stumbled and fell, bleeding from deep wounds in her rump and belly.

The discovery of a wolf kill in the woods seldom fails to have an emotional impact on the human mind. The snow is padded down with tracks, coming and going over several days of feasting. It is easy to over-estimate the number of wolves and it does not require much imagination to think that the woods are full of them. To some people the implication of the gory discovery seems clear: "No wonder there are so few moose...!"

The idea that predators constitute serious competition for human hunters has been around for centuries and is still argued passionately today, in the glow of campfires as well as in the rarefied atmosphere of universities. What are the facts? What is the true effect of wolf predation on a prey population? The question has been studied by biologists for half a century now, in laboratories and in the field. Millions of dollars have been spent on the charter of aircraft and the latest in technical gadgets, such as satellite radio-telemetry, that make it possible to determine exactly where wolves go and what they do. There is no lack of information. During the last two decades, a flood of hard data has been presented in an endless stream of reports, dissertations, papers, articles and books.

At the 1992 North American Symposium on Wolves, biologist Todd Fuller, who conducted intensive research on the population dynamics of deer in Minnesota, said that the wolf was the most studied large carnivore in the world. During the same meeting, biologist David Mech called it one of the most studied of all wild species. Yet, he ended his presentation with the following statement: "Despite all the long-term studies that are going on, the results are inconclusive...I am not sure we'll ever answer all the questions relating to the effects of wolf predation to completely satisfy everybody."

While it is to be expected that wolf biologists want to continue the ever more imaginative and sophisticated research effort, most wildlife managers agree that a broad understanding of the issues has begun to emerge. During the long process, there have been two complete reversals of thought on the most important question: Do wolves limit and regulate their prey? The pendulum of expert opinion has swung from yes to no and back again over the past twenty years. Ironically, current thinking about this principal question is very close to the ideas presented half a century ago by the first biologist who took to the field to do an objective study on wolves. His name was Adolph Murie.

His three-year project began in 1939 and took place in Denali National Park, Alaska. The park management had told Murie that an increase in wolves had given rise to official concern for the Dall sheep, the white thinhorns of the northern mountains. According to available estimates, their number had declined in the park from several thousand to about 1,500. What was the relationship between wolf and sheep?

A down-to-earth field biologist, Murie did not set out with some preconceived hypothesis. What he needed were the basic facts. First of all, he wanted to know which individuals in the prey population were dying. In those days before the invention of radio-collars, the only way to collect such information was through hard and painstaking fieldwork. During the short summer period, when the hills were free of snow, Murie and his assistant conducted a thorough search of sheep habitat. In total, he collected 829 skulls, an amazing number indeed!

After careful examination of tooth wear in the skulls, he

determined that the majority belonged to old sheep, those over nine years. There had also been a heavy mortality of young sheep in their first winter. Together, these age classes made up about 90 percent of the total sample. Of course, from just looking at the skulls, Murie could not tell whether or not the sheep had actually been killed by the wolves, but he assumed that most of them had. According to Murie, the above data constituted solid evidence that the wolves were preying mainly on the weak classes of their prey, on the old and the juveniles. But there was more...

Very few sheep that died were in their prime, between two and eight years of age, and the majority (68 percent) in this class showed signs of disease. How could Murie tell by just looking at an old skull? The jaws of these animals were deformed by necrosis, which is caused by a fungus. The organism gets a chance to invade the jaw of the living animal through abrasions or wounds caused by eating course vegetation, such as the sharp awns of certain grasses. An affected bone rots away or becomes enlarged and spongy. The teeth may eventually drop out or grow at abnormal angles. The mandibles are sometimes bent or almost severed. For ungulates, the chewing of cud is vital in order to obtain the nutrients out of their forage. Thus, any injury to the teeth becomes a serious handicap. Individuals that are badly afflicted by jaw bone disease are destined to decline in physical condition. If the herd is chased by a wolf, which sheep would be the first to be pulled down?

"Perhaps we should expect wolf predation to operate in this way," writes Murie. "For prey-predator relationships between large animals must be rather finely adjusted from the standpoint of species' preservation. The wolf and the sheep have existed together for a long time, so that an adjustment between them, whereby both can survive, should be expected... In mountain habitats, the wolf catches a few of the strong animals but preys mainly on the weak members of the population."

To Murie the relationship seemed necessary and logical, but he acknowledged that his idea was not new. Belief in the "survival of the fittest" was already popular among naturalists of the time. It was a cornerstone of the theory of natural selection proposed by Charles Darwin in 1859. Although Murie hesitated to say much about wolf predation as an evolutionary force on the sheep as a species, he contended that it might function most effectively in the selection of lambs. Healthy lambs were probably more likely to survive than weaklings. The wolf also caused the sheep to dwell in a rocky habitat where they were relatively safe from enemies. Another significant conclusion was that wolf predation was "the most important limiting factor in stabilizing sheep numbers and holding them in check."

Here we have, in a nutshell, the case for *Canis lupus* as it is widely accepted today. Wolves kill mostly the old, the very young and the infirm. By keeping up their selective pressure, wolves maintain prey population in a healthy state and in dynamic balance with habitat and food supplies. However, it cannot be denied that wolves sometimes take healthy prey, that they may kill more than they can eat, and that their methods are not always what we might call "humane."

These negative points are often glossed over or ignored by wolf defenders in the heated controversy that continues to swirl around the animal. However, it is important to take the wolf as it is, as objectively as we can, if we want to gain a deeper understanding of the role of predation. We cannot admire the wild hunters for their beauty and forget the killing that sustains them. The finer details of the interaction between predator and prey are exactly what makes wolf observation in the wild so fascinating.

How do wolves actually kill their prey? What hunting methods do they use? How do seemingly defenceless creatures such as deer cope with their powerful arch enemy lurking in the woods? What are the strategies used by elk and moose to protect their helpless new-born? These are questions that fascinate the wolf watcher. But all too seldom do we get a first-hand glimpse of what really goes on in the wild, hidden from view by trees or the darkness of night. It is a red-letter day when we, by sheer luck or perseverance, finally are witness at the kill, when we happen to be in the right place at the right time. But we may not necessarily enjoy all that we see...

Strung out in full flight, the elk herd runs up the open hillside above the lower Athabasca valley. The group contains mostly cows, yearlings and a few calves. Suddenly, as if she had forgotten something, one of the leading females turns around and trots back downhill, bleating anxiously. She sees the two humans standing on the edge of the grassy slope. Unafraid, she approaches closely, hackles up and nostrils flaring. Then she veers away and continues downhill, agitated, calling all the while. What is she looking for? Her calf! But there will be no answer to her call. Never again will the calf come bounding up to its mother in its playful way...

When the wolves chased the elk through the woods and across the shallow river channels, the calf was in the rear of the herd. Closely pursued, it splashed into a beaver pond but found no escape. The wolves followed it into the water and grabbed it from behind. Ripping and tugging, they dragged their bleeding prey to the bank, pulling it up between golden willows.

Red meat soon lies steaming in the frosty autumn air. Ravens that saw the kill wait in the trees, cawing to each other excitedly. High above, a migrating golden eagle interrupts its journey and circles in the azure sky, watching. Half an hour later, the wolves leave already, gorged with food. In the woods by the river, the cow elk is still bleating and searching. When she finally finds her dead calf, she stands guard over the remains, her agony heart-rending to behold.

When elk are pursued and hard-pressed by wolves, their major escape route usually leads to water. The predators may give up the chase right there, but if they are persistent, they wade or swim after their prey, continuing the chase on the other side of the river or lake. If the wolves really mean business, they will not hesitate to attack in the water and the elk's only hope lies in finding a channel of deep turbulence where its long legs allow it to stand while a wolf loses its footing.

When lakes and ponds are frozen, elk find a last refuge in the swiftest rivers where some stretches stay open all winter. Some animals that have been attacked, perhaps with severe wounds inflicted to the rear, are so desperate that they plunge into water holes where the wolves do not dare to follow. They pace up and down the shore or lie down for a snooze. The wounded elk is forced to stand in the freezing water until it cools off to the point of no return. Even if the wolves leave after a few hours, the sharp edge of the ice will make the elk's exit difficult. A calf or even the biggest bull may end up freezing into the ice. Not until late March when the carcass begins to thaw out of its deep-freeze tomb, do wolves and other scavengers get a chance to feed on it, just before the remains are swept downstream by the torrents of spring.

Over much of North America, the wolf's major food is deer, either the white-tailed or the mule deer, or both. Even in Jasper where several other species of ungulates, such as elk and mountain sheep, are more numerous, deer are the wolf's optimum prey on a year-round basis. This has several reasons. Firstly, deer are widely distributed in all forested and semi-open habitats. Secondly, in contrast to adult moose and elk which are capable of putting up a fierce fight when cornered, deer are easily killed, even for a single wolf. How does a deer, this elegant and harmless prince of the woods, cope with an aggressor as dangerous as the wolf that lurks in the dark and may be stalking closer at any moment? The first line of defense is to discover your enemies before they spot you. In the deer, this instinctive quality has been honed to perfection over eons of evolutionary time. As biologist David Henry once put it, predator and prey have been embroiled in an ongoing arms race; while the wolf developed speed and strength to overcome its prey, the deer improved its defenses and ability to escape.

The deer's sight may be poor, but in the woods, sharp eyes are of minor value and perhaps even a hindrance, especially at dusk when stumps and stones take on the shape of lurking beasts. If a deer had as much imagination as a human being, it might see a wolf behind every tree! Day or night, this much hunted creature is at peace in the gloomiest woods and goes about its business blissfully unaware of the scenery. Nibbling on leaves and twigs, delicately picking a flower or bud, a deer may approach you closely without recognizing your still form as a potential threat. Unless you move! And unless the deer smells or hears you. Finely honed, these senses constitute the deer's early warning system. The merest sound or whiff of wolf may send it flying through the air with the grace of a ballerina. Before the wolf knew it was there, the deer will be well on its way to safety, escaping easily by virtue of its championship at hurdles and its intimate knowledge of the terrain.

But what the wolf may lack in speed, it makes up in brute force and perseverance. Wolf packs often hunt in a line abreast through the woods, like a dragnet that may be more than a kilometer wide. If deer are flushed, they may unwittingly flee on a course that leads to the center of the line. Wolves on the flanks close in and cut off escape. Deer are especially vulnerable on a downhill chase which inhibits their high bounding gait. A deer jumping at full tilt down a steep slope risks falling or even breaking legs. By contrast, wolves rush down impetuously at break-neck speeds, over and through bushes, in flying leaps of up to ten meters (30 feet). Some deer are caught very quickly, taken by surprise at close range.

The prey's chances are affected favorably by snow cover if it is deep and loose. Mule deer bouncing along in their peculiar stiff-legged gait meet with minimal drag while the wolves are forced to plow through up to their bellies. On the other hand, snow works for the pursuer if there is a hard crust that holds a big-footed wolf but not a deer.

Like elk, deer instinctively flee to water which provides escape during summer. When you see a deer swim a lake or river, keep an eye on the bank where it came from. There may be a wolf on its trail! During winter, deer continue to run to water bodies, perhaps as a matter of habit or perhaps as a way of seeking the better footing afforded by ice. But ice is also slippery! Accidental falls, or floundering in soft spots and snowdrifts are the undoing for many deer, no matter how fit and healthy they may be.

Ice also provides good footing to wolves! In the lake-studded woodlands of eastern Canada and Minnesota, many deer chased by wolves are captured on frozen lakes. The open terrain allows wolves to actually see their prey and to cut corners. For instance, if the deer crosses a wide expanse of ice in a straight line and suddenly finds its path blocked by a cliff on the opposite shore, it is forced to change direction, which gives its pursuers an opportunity to head it off. Traveling on the wooded shores of large frozen lakes, wolves habitually drive deer toward the ice.

In the forest, wolves hunt down deer by scent, following fresh trails with nose to the ground. Lone wolves that lack the advantage of cooperative pack strategy compensate with perseverance, with dogged pursuit. Once they flush a deer, they may keep up the chase for miles, until the prey makes a fatal mistake, meets with an accident, or makes its escape....

One winterday in Jasper Park, a mule deer doe came running along a ridge trail toward me and hesitated just a few meters away. Panting and glassy-eyed, it stood a moment before continuing its flight, passing by at arm's length. Suspecting that it was being chased, I quickly stepped aside to the base of a spruce tree. Seconds later, a lone gray wolf came galloping along the trail, red tongue lolling over white fangs. It turned around in a flash when it became aware of the human presence.

In another case, a white-tailed buck ran by below an open ridge through woods covered with deep crusty snow. The deer's mouth was open and its tongue protruding. Peter DeMulder had stayed behind at the other end of the ridge, about a kilometer away. Unaware of his presence, the deer ran by him closely, looking exhausted and disoriented. At the base of a hill, it crashed through bushes instead of going around. It slipped and fell on a patch of ice, remaining prone for a full minute, licking its front foot which was bleeding, probably cut by the snow. Presently, the buck got up and resumed his flight. In the meantime, the pursuing wolf had seen me and halted at the other end of the ridge. Lying down for a rest, he was looking at me with an expression on his face that seemed to reveal his utter disgust or disappointment.

An exceptional observation of a long chase, which took place on a November day in Minnesota, was described in the *Journal of Mammalogy*. The wolf involved was radio-collared and under observation by researchers in a small aircraft. Together with three companions, the wolf flushed a white-tailed doe shortly after noon. The pack was about 40 meters (45 yards) behind and soon dropped back farther. While the others gave up, the radio-collared animal kept up the pursuit for over two hours, through spruce bogs, over hardwood ridges and across frozen lakes. Once the wolf got within five meters; at other times it was as much as 800 meters (900 yards) behind. At 14:20 p.m., when the plane had to return to base, the wolf was still following the deer's trail. At this point, the chase was almost 21 km (13 miles) from its starting point. The ultimate end, whether or not the deer was finally caught, was never determined.

Once overtaken, deer are easily killed by wolves. Yet it has seldom been witnessed by people, perhaps because it happens so quickly. One observer who saw a wolf spring after a deer in Jasper described it thus: "Just one bite' to the head. That was all." Mercifully efficient, the dispatch of deer stands in glaring contrast to the pulling down of large prey, particularly moose. Several wolf researchers have seen kills from the air and described their observations in clinical terms in zoological publications. As long as an adult moose stands its ground, the attack may be aborted. But an animal that flees, perhaps feeling unfit or vulnerable, will be pursued and harassed from behind. A bite in the lower belly can tear the skin and let out the guts. If the animal slows down to face its attackers, one of the wolves may grab it by the nose in a vise-like grip, holding on even if it is lifted bodily off the ground and shaken from side to side. In the meantime, other wolves slash the prey's hind quarters and may begin eating before the prey is dead.

In defense of their calves, moose have sent wolves packing with mortal blows of their sharp hooves. But many a courageous cow has been killed together with her calf. A stand-off by a defiant bull can take hours, or even days. After the first deep bites to the moose's rear, the wary attackers simply stand aside and let the animal weaken before approaching it again. In some instances, the pack leaves to hunt other prey, returning later to their earlier victim which may have succumbed to its wounds.

In Jasper Park, a wolf pack of seven inflicted much visible damage to a big elk bull that retreated to the ice of the frozen Athabasca River, where he stood or lay down for three days. His rump and upper hind legs were raw. One of his nostrils was ripped and looked like a loose flap of skin. The ice around was stained with blood and littered with hair. The wolves remained in the area, finishing the remains of another bull they had killed in the woods. Eventually, park warden Wes Bradford took pity on the bull and put him out of his misery. Next morning, the wolves were feeding, innocent and playful as children.

Like us, the wolf is a creature of contrasts. Its family life creates a picture that warms our heart but its foraging methods may shock us sometimes as cruel, a subjective value that is in the eye of the beholder. The wolf is certainly not a prudent predator. It does not argue, like modern conservationists, that elk and moose calves should be allowed to grow up before being "harvested". There is no question that wolves can inflict heavy mortality on new-born ungulates, but so did the native tribes in Canada's north. And their methods were no less cruel or inefficient than those of the large carnivores.

However, from the standpoint of wildlife conservation, the

wolf's timing in taking down old bulls is superior to human hunting. Trophy hunters often shoot male elk or moose in late summer or early autumn, before the rutting season has ended or even before it begins. By contrast, wolves pull the spent harem master down during winter, after he has finished his task of transmitting his master genes to the females. In natural systems, old bulls that escape wolf predation, may die anyway and end up as winterkill, even if they manage to hang on until spring. Nature has its own way of terminating the aged, through the grim harvesters of disease and starvation.

Whether maligned or beloved by us, the wolf is neither good nor bad. Predation is a drama that is older than the conscience of mankind. When the ancestors of "the naked ape" were just leaving the tropical forests, by the end of the Tertiary Period some three million years ago, the wolf already looked much like it does today: a successful cursorial hunter of hoofed animals, most of them much larger than itself.

In some respects, the early human tribes who chose to live on the plains and savannas of the northern hemisphere may have learned from and soon outdid wolves in preying on ungulates. No doubt, they clubbed as many helpless fawns and calves as they could. Ambushing animals larger than themselves, they killed by ganging up, by cooperation and by all available means. African aboriginals deliberately drove their spears into the rectum of an elephant and waited for their victim to succumb. In the same way, wolves tear at the flanks of a fleeing moose or elk, spilling its guts, and watching it die.

For wolves and primitive humans, the end justifies the means. The ultimate goal is always the same, culminating in the sacrifice of one creature and the survival of another.

Chapter 5

COMRADES AND COMPETITORS

The Chinook gusts over the wide expanse of Jasper Lake, shifting snowdrifts across the ice and rippling the surface of meltwater. Near the windward shore, it sweeps up freeze-dried silt that rises like a curtain of dust over the Canadian National Railway running along the lake. High over the hills beyond soars a bald eagle, in masterly command of the unruly updraught. Its white head is turned down, blinking in the sun. Slowly, it descends to the base of a bluff where a bighorn ewe was killed by the train during the night. Just as the eagle lowers its great yellow feet, a rabble of ravens bursts up from the ground, their raucous protest piercing the bluster of wind.

The lone black wolf, patrolling the opposite shore, pauses and stares intently across the lake. He does not know that there is a carcass by the sheep bluff, and far upwind he certainly would not be able to smell it. But the wolf has learned to associate ravens with carrion. If he is hungry he will come over to investigate. How will he get across the thawing lake? Let's sit down in the lee of some bushes to wait and see.

Are animals capable of abstract thought or are all their actions pre-programmed by instinct? It is a fundamental question that has engaged the minds of scientists and philosophers who have come to obtuse conclusions. Owners of house pets often have strong opinions inspired by first-hand observation of the clever behavior of their cat or dog. Animals may not be able to reason and calculate as we do, but there is little doubt that they are capable of learning, have excellent memories, strong emotions and perhaps even an intuition or sixth sense that is beyond our realm. In his book *The World of the Wolf*, Douglas Pimlott, who owned a dog and a pet wolf, writes: "My actions have so often been anticipated by these animals, in ways that I have not understood, that I cannot rule out the possibility that they enjoy mental processes beyond my comprehension."

The black wolf proceeds to cross the ice into the direction of the sheep hills on the other side of Jasper Lake, which is actually a shallow widening of the Athabasca River. Channels may open up at any time during winter when the Chinook blows and the temperature warms. The wolf does not get very far; an area of swift water blocks the way and he returns to shore, trots upstream a little ways, then ventures out onto the ice again. Once more he encounters open water. He tries again farther down with the same result. Abruptly, he now turns back and goes the other way along the shore, past the point where he began his crossing attempt, and heads directly to the lake's outlet, some distance away. A herd of elk standing on the flats nervously watches his approach and runs into the woods, ignored by the wolf.

At the outflow, the Athabasca River is deep and free of ice. Without hesitation, the animal enters the water, swims across the fast current, hauls out on the other side and vigorously shakes his fur. Then, without another pause, he travels directly to the sheep hills.

Interestingly, the wolf behaved exactly as I would have done when confronted with the treacherous lake during winter. If a safe route over the ice cannot be found, I abandon the risky attempt and cross the open outlet by canoe or dinghy. For me, the decision is based on intelligent reasoning. So why not for a wolf?

While we watch from our vantage point, the black wolf reaches the base of the hills, not exactly at the spot where the ravens and the eagle are, but a few hundred meters away. He ascends the slope and disappears from view behind a belt of trees. Presently, he emerges by the bluff downwind from the dead sheep, his final approach slow and alert.

Once again, the wolf has made a move that makes sense, or so it seems. A direct approach would have carried the risk of blundering into trouble. The carcass might have been tampered with by humans, or perhaps there were other large carnivores nearby. However, caution is instinctive for mammals that live by their noses. The ingrained habit of smell-before-you-act is reinforced by experience, by the simple fact that there are other creatures in this wilderness that are not necessarily friendly to wolves, especially a lone one.

For any scavenger, it is of critical importance to be on guard and check out a carcass before touching it. Predators are aggressive and may even prey on each other. No matter how powerful and agile, even wolves have enemies besides their own kind: bears and cougars. Their shared taste for venison often brings them in contact with each other. How do these armed competitors coexist and avoid bloodshed? And how does the wolf interact with the smaller carrion eaters that steal from its kills? Let's continue our watch at the railway bluff.

The wolf's initial inspection of the dead sheep is very brief and he leaves after a few minutes, disappearing into the hills. Returning by evening, he drags the carcass farther out onto the lake, pulling and tearing off chunks of meat and gristle that are chewed and swallowed. He ignores the ravens that surround him, calling querulously and snatching morsels just out of his reach. He departs quite soon again, leaving the birds in sole possession of the left-overs. They reclaim the carcass eagerly, hammering and drilling with their sharp beaks at frozen tissue where the shearing molars of the big carnivore have opened up the tough skin.

Ravens and wolves are comrades in their quest to wrench a living from the wilderness. During the day, the birds keep an eye on the traveling pack, losing contact during the long night. Early each winter morning, mated pairs of ravens leave their roost to patrol the valleys, one flying quite far apart from the other, croaking frequently in long-range communication. It is certain that their vocabulary of several dozen different calls contains a special sound to denote wolf. On Isle Royale in Lake Superior, ravens have been seen to follow wolf tracks. The island's two or three packs have been intensively studied for over thirty years. On winter mornings, the researchers fly a light aircraft along the island shoreline to locate wolves from the air. New snow is a great help to find out where the pack went during the night. Ravens operate the same way, winging steadily along a fresh trail to catch up with their benefactors, occasionally landing to pick apart a scat.

A wolf pack at its kill is soon attended by ten or more of the lively black rascals. To the watcher, it seems obvious that mammal and bird enjoy teasing and playing with each other. Sneaking up from behind, ravens may tug the tail of a pup, which cannot resist rushing the birds off their feet. Adults sometimes jump up high and attempt to snatch a low flying bird out of the air, rarely succeeding. Ravens are smart enough to know what wolves are doing when they carry off chunks of meat to be buried in the snow for later use. After the animal turns away, the crafty bird quietly descends on the spot, digging with its bill to uncover the cache. The raven survives in the wintry wilderness by its wits and by the involuntary cooperation of its canid comrade.

Wolf kills are important for many other wilderness animals. For some they constitute a bonanza of cold-weather protein, for others just emergency rations. Eagles, rough-legged hawks and even gyrfalcons profit during lean times. Magpies, jays and chickadees chip off what they can eat and carry away. Mammals, such as foxes, martens and weasels, have the added advantage of smelling out hidden riches with their food-finding noses. All of these free-loaders have access to the wolf's larder because of its habit of departing for a snooze between meals. If their immediate hunger is satisfied, wolves leave left-overs in the open and seek a resting place some distance away. By contrast, the table manners of the big cats are quite different, allowing little room for altruistic contributions to the community. Let us resume our watch at the sheep bluff...

When we return next morning, we find that the carcass has disappeared. The freshly fallen snow holds the footprints of the wolf but also of a mountain lion, the secretive feline of the west, called cougar or puma. Its tracks are not quite as large as those of a wolf and show no imprint of nails. Moreover, the cat's foot is somewhat crooked with a relatively larger heel pad, and the step is shorter with more straddle. As indicated by sign, the cougar dragged the remains of the ewe back to the shore and across the railway to the base of the hills. Following the fresh marks in the snow, we approach a dense stand of young spruce. Suddenly, a matter of meters away, the cougar bolts out of cover, bounding up the steep slope above and out of sight over the rimrock. When we recover from the surprise, we investigate the area and find the carcass in a depression under bushes. It is the way of the puma; hide your food, lie up nearby and guard it against all others.

Later during the day, the black wolf and the cougar walk across the open hillside, a few body lengths apart, each keeping a wary eye on the other. Suddenly, the cat darts at its long-legged companion that dodges easily. From a distance, as viewed through binoculars, it looks as if the odd couple are playing. But for a predator it is a thin line that separates play from deadly aggression. A wolf, radio-collared by Alberta biologists and belonging to a pack that denned inside Jasper National Park, was actually killed by a cougar and bitten through the head. In Glacier Park, a radio-collared wolf pack tracked by Montana researchers encountered a three-months-old cougar kitten and left nothing but skin and bones.

Not much is known about the interaction of wolves and the much smaller wildcat of the northwoods, the Canada lynx. A Jasper park warden once observed that a lynx took over a sheep carcass from a yearling wolf, which did not get a chance to feed over several days while the shaggy cat monopolized the carrion. However, if challenged by a pack, a prudent lynx would certainly run for the safety of trees.

Wolves and mustelids, members of the weasel family, do not get along too well either. Even the wolverine, which has a reputation for ferocity greatly exceeding its true, retiring nature, had better run at the approach of the pack. There are a few records that this big weasel was actually intercepted and killed. Wolves also destroy any marten, mink, ermine or otter they can catch, leaving the meat mostly uneaten. But members of their own clan, foxes and coyotes, are not treated any better.

At best, the three wild dogs coexist by an uneasy truce in their running battle. They steal from each other's kills and caches, with lethal risks for the smaller species. About half the size of a wolf,

coyotes pose direct competition by preying on deer and sheep, especially the young. Lacking the powerful jaws of the larger predator, the coyote kills ungulates by suffocation, grabbing a fawn or lamb by the throat in a choke-hold. A pair of aggressive coyotes may not fear a lone wolf and grudgingly make way at the carcass. But if adult wolves rush out of cover, the interlopers have to flee for their life. Many a dead coyote, partly eaten or still largely intact, has been found in Jasper and elsewhere. On Isle Royale, coyotes became extirpated about eight years after wolves reached the island, crossing frozen Lake Superior from neighboring Canada. Yellowstone's coyotes were hit hard after wolves became reestablished. However, in most regions where wolf country borders on settled lands, coyote populations can maintain themselves because of dispersal and immigration from adjacent wolf-free territory where their densities may be very high.

In turn, coyotes chase and kill foxes, especially the pups. In the mountains, Reynard has learned to avoid his aggressive cousin by sticking to the hills while the coyote dominates the lower valleys. The red fox, being so much lighter than either of his cousins, is very nimble on steep terrain and snowdrifts, has a small range and hunts mainly mice and squirrels. Therefore, it generally avoids the wolf and does not compete with it directly. By virtue of their differences, the two species have coexisted for millennia over their vast common breeding range. A hungry fox may take advantage of a wolf kill, confident in its speed to get away if the owners come back. Yet, some of these furry freeloaders may get caught by surprise, the slender body shaken and mangled, their bushy tail cut off, just for sport.

The animal in which wolves meet their match is the bear. Disputes over kills between grizzlies and wolf packs have often been observed in the open tundra of Alaska by air-borne biologists. It is a tug of war that may go either way. Less agile and often outnumbered, the big brute may throw his weight around to no avail. Dashing in and out, one wolf may nip him in the rear while others engage him at the front. Grumbling and grunting terribly, the biggest grizzly may give up the fight if the wolves are determined. The most serious encounters between grizzlies and wolves take place around dens. Adolph Murie observed an incident in Denali National Park after a female bear with three lusty yearlings approached a wolf den from downwind. They paused, lifting their noses, perhaps smelling cached meat, and got very close before they were noticed by four wolves that had been fast asleep. When they dashed to the attack, the young bears seemed to enjoy the fight. One of them would charge the wolves vigorously, occupying much of their attention while mother bear poked about, uncovering and feeding on meat scraps the wolves had buried. The foursome remained at the den for an hour before finally moving off.

Bear visits to wolf home-sites can have fatal consequences for the pups. In June of 1976, Yukon biologists Bob Hayes and Dave Mossop observed a battle royal involving a sow and two big cubs that were digging at a den defended by seven wolves. As the helicopter swung close, the bears ran off, pursued by the wolves. Charges and counter charges flew. At one point, a wolf bit the shoulder of a yearling and was dragged for some distance before letting go. The biologists saw a similar incident four years later. And in July of 1989, they found evidence that bears had dug into the den and actually killed and eaten four pups. The remains of wolf pups eaten by predators have also been found in Jasper, where it is common to see black bears or their sign near wolf home-sites. Adult wolves have been found as victims of black bears in Algonquin Park as well as in Alaska.

As if to revenge themselves, wolves sometimes kill bears. There is at least one report of a fatal encounter between a pack and a yearling grizzly in Alaska. In Denali, a sow with four small cubs was surrounded by 17 aggressive wolves which killed and ate three of the hapless youngsters. There are several records of wolf predation on black bears. A most grisly case occurred on December 19, 1982, and was published in the *Canadian*

Field-Naturalist. During an aerial survey of moose in northern Alberta, a team of biologists happened to come across a site where a pack of eight wolves had made a recent kill. The men landed their helicopter to investigate and found pieces of skin and two paws of a black bear. The victim had apparently been hibernating in a shallow winter den under the roots of a willow bush. The wolves had dug out the animal and killed it some distance away. The most pathetic casualties of the encounter were two bear cubs which the observers found clinging to the top of a poplar tree. The following day, the cubs were on the ground and the wolves had gone. The report included no further information on the eventual fate of the orphans.

Whether or not wolves have the ability to think and make decisions based on reasoning is an intriguing question that remains open for debate and continued observation. But it is a fact of life that their interaction with other creatures has nothing to do with our sense of fairness and moral judgement. A wolf's aggressive behavior may not always be motivated by its immediate needs, but certainly not by malice, hatred or skewed fear, as is so often the case in the human species.

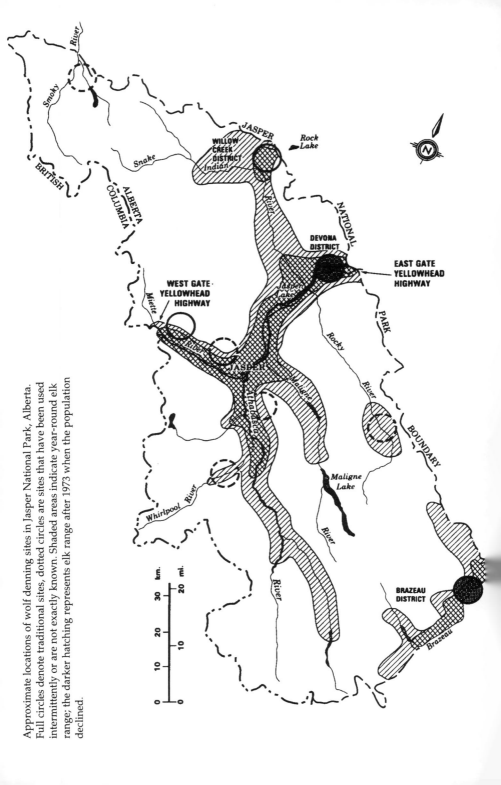

Approximate locations of wolf denning sites in Jasper National Park, Alberta. Full circles denote traditional sites, dotted circles are sites that have been used intermittently or are not exactly known. Shaded areas indicate year-round elk range; the darker hatching represents elk range after 1973 when the population declined.

Chapter 6

THE NOT-SO-NATURAL HISTORY OF JASPER

From the entrance of the Pocahontas Cave, on the lower slopes of the Bosche Range, we see the valley as the stone-age inhabitants must have seen it. Below, the Athabasca River meanders down its alluvial bottomlands, a mosaic of woods and montane meadows. On either side, rocky mountains stand shoulder to shoulder, descending in height to the east and ascending to snow-capped giants in the southwest, glaringly white in the hot summer sky.

Over millions of years, while the towering ramparts of Roche Miette have stood sentinel over the valley, great changes have taken place here. During the ice ages, glaciers pushed up to the highest peaks, scouring and carving the spaces between into u-shaped basins that roared with torrents of meltwater during the ice's retreat. But during the relatively recent period after the first humans arrived, the landscape has not changed much, except that forests now cover formerly open terrain.

The cave stands empty now, rarely visited by people. Still visible on the flat surface above the entrance is the mark of a hand, printed in red-ochre paint that has deeply stained the porous limestone. Archaeologists digging into the debris inside the vault-like cavern have unearthed a few crude stone tools and bone splinters of hoofed mammals that date back four or five thousand years. Of much more recent origin are the pellets of bighorn sheep that litter the floor, and in a gritty corner is a scrape where a cougar has buried its scat.

Today, the valley is a paradise for wildlife, a vital wintering habitat for herds of sheep and elk, as well as for their predators. But what was it like in the old days when the cave was occupied? What impact did the primitive peoples have on the fauna? Very little is known for sure. The stone-age tribes did not leave a written record. Probably, they were skilled hunters who had learned the ways of the wolf and used cooperative strategies to ambush grazing animals and drive them to very low numbers in this strategic valley. Perhaps the families were forced to subsist mainly on berries, roots or fish. However, moving their camp often, they may have had little lasting impact on the diversity and density of large mammals over the larger region. However, it is certain that an abrupt change took place during the early 1700s with the arrival of bands of Indians from eastern Canada.

Displaced by the "white man's" conquest of Ontario and Quebec, parties of Iroquois, Stoneys and Crees paddled their birch bark canoes far up the great western rivers, across the prairies to the imposing front ranges of the Rocky Mountains. Armed with rifles and metal knives, obtained from European traders, the newcomers waged war on their stone-age brothers along the way. They also hunted hoofed mammals and furbearers with deadly persistence. In 1811, when the intrepid David Thompson had the dubious honor of being the first European to venture through the Athabasca valley, primeval conditions had long since passed into unrecorded history. Thompson and his Indian guides made their arduous journey, on the way to the Pacific west coast, in the dead of winter and they saw very little game. A few years later, the valley became a regular travel corridor for fur brigades, bringing up trade supplies by canoe all the way from Montreal and taking rich cargoes of beaver, marten and otter back east for shipment to Britain and France. In 1814, fur traders built a post in the valley, Jasper House, named after one of the early occupants. Although the company men brought packs of pemmican and other food staples with them, their staff as well as most private travelers augmented their supplies with venison and fish whenever the opportunity arose.

In the late 1820s, Jasper House was manned by a Scot named Michael Klyne. According to one of his visitors, he was "a jolly old fellow" who lived with an Indian woman and a large family in "a miserable concern of rough logs." Klyne's unpublished diaries, preserved in the archives of the Hudson's Bay Company, paint a grim picture of wildlife conditions in the valley. During winter, his full-time Metis hunter made extensive foraging trips in the surrounding country but often returned with nothing, sometimes without having seen a single track. Additional proof that game was scarce can be inferred from Klyne's frequent references to hungry Indians who came to the post to barter beaver skins. By early March of 1830, three families of Shuswaps arrived at the post. "They are starving all the time." On March 25, a Shuswap arrived "almost dead of starving. I gave him a little meat to eat for himself and a little to take to his family. I cannot give him much. I have little myself. In the evening my hunter arrived. Saw nothing."

On April 10, a Shuswap woman showed up at Klyne's post with three children. "A few days past, two other children and her husband died of hunger." Two weeks later, during the night, the Shuswap woman departed, leaving two of her children at Jasper House. Klyne described the tragedy in very few words. "I sent after her to come for her children but no-one could find her track."

Hunting pressure on the wildlife resources of the Jasper area was not confined to the major travel route through the Athabasca valley. The Indians and Metis of that era were a footloose kind who ventured far into the mountains in search of beaver, living off the land and shooting game wherever they found it. Michael Klyne wrote that so-called "freemen" rode by Jasper House with many pack horses on the way up the long valley of the Snake Indian River, a tributary of the Athabasca, and beyond. Postmasters who came after Klyne used horses in a big way to supply the post with wild meat. During the mid 1800s, John Moberley led parties of 80-100 people with 150 horses over the pitching trails in the foothills. On one of his extended expeditions, the party killed over 70 moose, besides caribou, sheep and goats. But no elk!

In fact, elk which are so common now, were already scarce when Klyne began his service at Jasper House. During the entire winter of 1830-1831, his hunter saw only three red deer, as he called them, of which two were shot. It is not hard to understand why elk were easy targets for meat hunters; they live in herds and prefer open country, especially during winter when they concentrate in the lower valleys. By contrast, moose are loners and far less vulnerable, thinly spaced throughout their forested habitat. Bighorn sheep are a herding animal too, with a preference for open slopes, but the species has a wider distribution than elk and retreats to rugged alpine terrain in spring and summer.

During the latter half of the 1800s, as more and more trappers, prospectors and miners came to the West, meat hunting intensified and led to increasing scarcity of all large ungulates. By the turn of the century, which was marked by extremely severe winters, large mammals reached their lowest point. Although a few are believed to have survived along the remote Brazeau River, elk had been practically exterminated in all of the Alberta mountains and foothills.

What about wolves? Their historic abundance, decline and recovery are closely tied to that of the elk. During his winters at Jasper House, Michael Klyne wrote that wolves occasionally killed a few of the company horses that wintered in the valley. To protect their stock, postmasters set out poison baits as early as 1859. During the latter part of the century, wolves were apparently rare in all of the region, partly because of poisoning but mainly as an indirect result of the great scarcity of their prey species, the hoofed mammals.

The concept of conservation did not take hold in the West until the beginning of the new century. Jasper National Park was established in 1907. Within its 10,880 km² (4,200 miles²) of mountains and valleys, ungulates were finally protected from the gun and began a slow recovery. Elk were reintroduced in 1920 when 88 animals were shipped in from Yellowstone National Park. They multiplied quickly to 1,000-1,200 in 1926, and to about 3,000 in the early 1940s. But then another problem arose: overpopulation!

Suitable elk wintering habitat, grassy meadows and slopes, are of limited extent in the Athabasca valley and had to be shared with bighorn sheep and several hundred head of outfitter horses that were allowed to winter in the park. Overgrazing and large-scale destruction of browse were noted by several researchers who recommended culling of the elk herds. Beginning in 1942, wardens shot and butchered up to 300 animals each winter, mostly females. The drastic measure was designed to dampen the herd's breeding potential and to alleviate grazing pressure on the winter range. It remained in effect until 1970 when such artificial reductions were no longer deemed appropriate in a national park. Fortunately, by that time other great changes had begun to take place in Jasper, changes that would eventually lead to a better balance on the winter range. One of them was a ban on horse grazing. The second and perhaps the most important was a return of the elk's natural predators.

Already in the 1930s, while the numbers of elk and other ungulates were building, wolves had made a come-back, perhaps dispersing from the great wilderness to the north. Unfortunately, their return was seen with misgivings by park staff and they were shot on sight. By the late 1930s, wolves were denning in the Athabasca valley and packs were seen in the backcountry in all of the major drainages. What effect were the predators having on the park's game herds? This pressing question was put to Ian McTaggart-Cowan, who later became the dean of Canadian zoologists, and who was at the time conducting a series of ungulate studies in the western parks. His wolf study ran from 1943 to 1946 and constitutes the first official research project on the species undertaken in Canada. His report was published in the *Canadian Journal of Research* and is a very readable document that is still relevant today.

Based on information provided by wardens, Cowan estimated the number of wolves in the park at a minimum of 35 and a maximum of 55. To find out what they were killing, tracks were followed in winter and scats collected throughout the year. Examined in a laboratory through a microscope, the hairs of food items contained in the scats could be identified as to species, giving a reasonably accurate picture as to the diet of the predators. Based on his analysis, Cowan estimated that at least 47 percent of the wolf's food consisted of elk. The proportion of calf hairs in the scats were about equal to adult remains, reflecting a relatively high take of calves. Yet, Cowan found "no discernible difference in the survival of young" in elk herds with or without predators. Apparently, elk productivity in the park was low overall, due to the poor foraging conditions. By December, no more than 18 percent of cows had surviving calves. At the end of his investigation, Cowan concluded that the wolves were "not detrimental to the park game herds, and that their influence was definitely secondary, in the survival of game, to the welfare factors, of which the absence of sufficient suitable winter forage is the most important."

In his report, Cowan reiterated park management views that the winter ranges, which the elk shared with sheep and deer, were severely overgrazed. Moreover, the starving herds were damaging poplar stands to the detriment of beavers, which used to be abundant and an important summer food for the wolves.

For the next two decades, despite the yearly culling efforts by wardens, elk population estimates remained at much the same level as before, at 2,500-3,000, and range conditions did not improve. By the end of the 1960s, sheep biologist John Stelfox expressed serious concern that the bighorns were in poor physical condition and suffering from malnutrition. He warned that a serious disease might break out at any time, leading to devastation of the herds. Another species that was believed to be suffering from competition by elk was mountain caribou. Their numbers in the park were declining, while elk were invading caribou summer range on the alpine meadows.

Faced with all of these considerations, Ludwig Carbyn, a biologist with the Canadian Wildlife Service, began a wolf study in Jasper in 1969 designed as a research project for the requirements of a Ph.D. degree at the University of Toronto, supervised by Douglas Pimlott. Carbyn's study was to be conducted for the same length of time as Cowan's, about four years, and his specific goal was to examine the impact of wolf predation on elk.

Based on warden reports and his own observations in the Snake Indian drainage, Carbyn estimated the park's wolf population at 48-50. Using similar methodology as his predecessor, he calculated that the elk's share in the wolf's diet was 30 percent and that mule deer, at 43 percent, was the most common prey species. However, during early summer, wolf predation shifted from deer to elk calves as soon as they became available. Carbyn believed that "predation on calves could significantly influence elk populations by constantly reducing recruitment." Nevertheless, based on his data, he had to conclude that Jasper's wolves were not effective in controlling elk numbers. The reason, he said, had to do with the low densities of wolves.

It was a pity that his study was not carried on after 1972, for soon after Carbyn left Jasper, a major change began to unfold in the prey and predator dynamics of the entire region. During 1973-1975, elk declined in the park to less than half of former numbers while wolves doubled or tripled. The causes of the sudden shift in balance were several but the major factor that precipitated the change was weather. The winter of 1972-1973 was quite severe but 1973-1974 broke all records. At the end of January 1974, snow depth at Jasper was nearly one meter (three feet), and by the end of March still over half a meter. These were the highest levels in 45 years, since such statistics had been kept by Environment Canada.

Deep snow in combination with poor winter range is a double-edged calamity for elk with serious consequences that go beyond their own generation. The animals are forced to dig down to the ground with their front hooves and if the reward is only a few blades of grass or next to nothing, the gains do not compensate for the cost in energy. Moreover, poor nutrition of pregnant cows leads to low reproduction and weak calves that easily fall prey to predators, wolves as well as bears and cougars. Calves that manage to scrape through, eventually give birth to less than healthy calves which are again more vulnerable to predators than the progeny of well-fed mothers. Researcher David Mech has called this chain of impairment the "grandmother effect."

During the winter of 1973-1974, some elk in starved condition were shot by park staff to shorten their misery. The following year, Jasper's elk population was estimated at 850-1,000, roughly a third of what it had been before. The declines were more gradual than it seemed and had started after the cold winter of 1971-1972. The following summer, elk numbers had already dropped noticeably in some outlying districts, particularly at Willow Creek in the upper Snake Indian drainage. And the causes may have involved more than just starvation.

By comparison, based on warden service data, elk declines were greatest, up to 78-94 percent, in the outlying regions where elk herds migrated across park boundaries in fall onto provincial lands, where they were subject to hunting, with an open season that lasted from early September to late December. During the 1960s and early 1970s, there were no quotas on the number of female elk that could be shot in western Alberta. Although few figures are available, one official estimate of the hunting kill for the Brazeau region, on Jasper's eastern boundary, was 13 percent of the local population. The combined impact of overhunting, severe weather and poor range, superimposed on natural mortality, eventually resulted in the near-total destruction of elk at Willow Creek on Jasper's north boundary which had been the center of Carbyn's study area. The local herd of 120-150 dwindled to less than twenty. But there is little doubt that wolves played a role too.

Elk estimates also dropped steeply in areas where hunting did not take place at all, such as the main valley where declines were calculated at 60-70 percent. While the Athabasca valley herds stayed all year within the protection of the park, they were safe from the gun but subject to another hazard: traffic fatalities. Today, collisions with vehicles and trains kill a substantial proportion, six or seven percent, of the population in the lower valley. Prior to 1975, known accidental deaths were only two percent, an insignificant contribution to the great decline.

What had been the exact impact of wolf predation on the elk? The question posed by Cowan and Carbyn was even more urgent *after* the elk decline. Since the mid 1960s, released from decades of poisoning on adjacent provincial lands, wolves had multiplied in and outside the park, their reproduction boosted by plenty of vulnerable prey. In 1974, Jasper's wolf population was estimated at 80-100, double what it was before. In the Snake Indian River drainage, where Carbyn had located only one pack in 1969-1972, there were three denning packs in 1981. How were the remnant elk herds coping now? The answer would emerge, not by another short-term study, but over the long haul through the continued monitoring by park wardens and naturalists.

The interaction of elk and wolves has been studied in Jasper far longer than anywhere else in North America. Today, to the astute observer, it is soon evident that the presence of large predators has deeply influenced the behavior of the park's elk, especially cows with calves. Nowadays, more than half of the population remains all year near the townsite, in campgrounds or along major roads. This has two main reasons. One is the simple fact that some of the best open habitat for grazing animals is created and maintained by human developments. And secondly, like all prey species, elk are quick to take advantage of any situation that reduces the risk of predation. It is this deep and overriding instinct that makes elk seek the company of people, those two-legged, gawking but harmless creatures and their noisy machines. Elk have learned that big carnivores, particularly wolves, are relatively scarce in human-activity areas. During winter, up to 70 percent of all Jasper elk occur right along roads and near the town. In Banff National Park, after wolves made a big come-back during the late 1980s, the number of elk in the townsite increased noticeably. Rutting bulls and cows with new-born calves have become a menace in the town and on the golf course, attacking and even wounding people who venture too close.

Fortunately, there are still a few elk in the backcountry where the relationship with predators can be studied in a more natural setting. How do elk in the wilderness attempt to avoid predators? In the southern portion of Jasper and in adjacent Banff National Park, elk cows with calves retreat to high alpine solitudes during spring and summer, while wolves stay behind near their den sites in the lower regions. It is the same age-old strategy used by caribou and sheep.

In water-logged regions, such as the lower Athabasca valley, pregnant cows employ a similar anti-predator strategy as deer and moose; they isolate themselves on islands between fast-flowing river channels and hide their new-born in dense vegetation. Still, they need luck to avoid detection by the sharp senses of wolves and bears that patrol the river banks and undoubtedly know a lot more about the habits of their prey than we do.

If attacked, mother elk defend their small calves fearlessly. With a well-placed blow of a front hoof, she is capable of splitting a wolf's skull. Working together, a nursery herd may be successful in driving off attackers, but if a lone elk cow is harassed by several wolves, her youngster is doomed. During fall and early winter, when the calves have grown to two-thirds of adult size, they are even harder to protect because they stray farther from their dam. When the herd flees, the wolves single out animals that are easiest to pull down, easiest to kill. Experienced and skilled at what they do, the wild hunters concentrate on calves as long as they can be found....

By late fall, elk herds in Jasper's wolf country usually have few young left but they are well protected. Cows with calves are extremely wary, near the front of the herd and first to flee if they receive a warning. At the sight of mortal danger, elk emit an explosive, squealing bark. If twenty or thirty adults run in compact formation, the few surviving young are obscured from view and shielded by a stampede of big bodies that send snow and dirt flying under flailing hooves.

If actually overtaken and cornered by wolves, a mature elk may stand its ground successfully, particularly if its backside is protected by a cliff or dense stand of trees. In the Athabasca valley, elk often use steep banks and promontories as a last refuge. Standing on the edge, they keep their vulnerable rump toward the precipice and face their attackers with hooves or antlers ready for a spirited defense. One such stand-off that I saw, lasted at least four and perhaps as long as eight hours before the yearling bull got away, perhaps helped by my involuntary interference.

During summer and fall, when they are in prime physical condition, mature elk bulls have little to fear from wolves and do not even bother to flee. Standing tall with massive antlers, looming over the wolves like prehistoric giants, they make threatening rushes at their cowering enemy. However, during winter, after the big bulls have been weakened by the rutting season, they feel far less gutsy and seek refuge in deep woods to escape attention. If they stay with the herd in the open, it is the spent harem master that would be selected for the kill if the wolves gave chase.

Elk, or wapiti as they are more correctly called, are grazers and essentially plains animals with good eyesight, as opposed to myopic forest dwellers such as moose and deer. During winter, herds of cows with their calves and yearlings, as well as some young bulls, like to dwell in open country so that they can see danger from afar. Both their preference for open terrain and their herding instinct are anti-predator strategies. For the individual, there is indeed safety in numbers; the more eyes, the quicker an enemy is spotted. In Jasper's backcountry, especially after they have been chased a few times, elk become extremely wary and run at the first sign of potential danger, people included. For this reason it is difficult to get a good look at a herd and to classify the age groups, to determine what percentage of calves has survived the critical months of spring and early summer. If we were to compare calf-cow ratios from the backcountry with areas near the townsite where wolves are few, such data could open up an interesting window on the essence of the question we are investigating, the question of the impact of wolf predation on elk.

In mid November from 1986 to 1991, park wardens conducted classified counts of elk along roads in the main valley and amassed a very large data sample of cows and calves, totalling 1,721 animals. From year to year, the percentage of calves per 100 cows varied from 43 to 61 and averaged 48. By comparison, counts taken in two outlying districts averaged 18 and 19 calves per 100 cows!

One of these two backcountry counts involved a sample of 425 animals obtained in July by personnel of the Alberta Fish and Wildlife Division, who conducted an intensive wolf study along the Brazeau River on the eastern border of Jasper Park in

1983-1986. Their four-year elk survey was flown by helicopter over the alpine summer range of an elk herd. In each of the first two years, the total count was 152 cows and calves. The percentage of calves per 100 cows was 25-33. Chances were that this ratio would drop during the course of the summer and fall. At the time of the census, the local wolf pack was still at the den at lower elevations along the Brazeau River. The pack would become more mobile later on, traveling up to the high country where the elk were.

During the last two years of the surveys, elk numbers had dropped and sample sizes were smaller at 72 and 49 with respective calf percentages of only 7 and 4. The researchers strongly suspected that these extremely low calf survival rates were directly linked to wolf predation. During the surveys, a wolf pack with pups was seen on the open slopes where the elk nursery herd was spending the summer. In one instance, the observers came upon them feeding on a freshly killed calf. Evidently, it had just been pulled down since the herd was still in flight.

Although the above evidence is largely circumstantial, it parallels data from the other backcountry district in the lower Athabasca valley where I obtained classified counts for ten winters during 1983-1992. In years when the local pack of 8-10 wolves was denning a few kilometers from the elk calving grounds, cow:calf ratios were lowest at 8 percent. In these years the wolves were seen to make direct trips to and from the river islands where the cows were hiding their calves. By contrast, during years when the wolf pack was small and spent less time in the area, the calf percentage varied between 15 and 30 percent. Although the sample size was low, in 1983 when the local wolf pack had disappeared, the percentage of calves was 76 percent! Moreover, elk herd size was correlated with wolf presence over the ten years of intensive observation. After a few years of low wolf numbers, the local herd increased from 30 to 61. It decreased again to 28 after four years of high wolf presence, and rebuilt once more to 52 after three low wolf years.

Of course, there are additional factors, particularly bear predation, that can depress elk recruitment. Throughout Jasper, grizzlies and blacks are common in all habitats, even along roadsides in the main valley, where both species have been seen to kill elk calves. Also cougars are known to prey on elk. Nevertheless, it is hard to deny that the most likely explanation for the low cow:calf ratios in the backcountry is wolf predation. Locally, it can have a severe impact because elk are quite scarce in Jasper's back woods and have a clumped distribution, while wolf packs tend to select dens near elk calving grounds.

However, this grim scenario should not be extrapolated over all of Jasper. Some elk may escape predation in localities away from regular wolf travel routes. Overall, the park's population is increasing and currently estimated at well over one thousand. In the main valley, elk are probably as numerous as they should be in view of available habitat; their favorite hang-outs are heavily cropped. Some wardens would favor a program of using fire in controlled burns to get rid of trees and make more meadow habitat available. Others prefer to let nature take its own course in the national park.

Here and there, a few elk are surviving in the backcountry, apparently coping better after hunting regulations have been tightened up on adjacent provincial lands. In the meantime, wolf numbers have readjusted as well. By 1983, their population was down to 27-50 and it has remained near that level for a dozen years, up to this day.

Great changes have also taken place on the elk winter ranges in the lower Athabasca valley near Devona. The formerly heavily overgrazed meadows have recovered. Especially after a wet growing season, tall plumes of grass wave in the Chinook. The ancient hills and bottomlands have sunk back in time, to the days before the white man arrived, when this scenic valley was an exclusive paradise to the tribe who left a hand print in red-ochre over the entrance of the Pocahontas cave.

Part II

FROM VARMINT
TO FAVORITE

Weary of cities and the wheeled machine,
we look to wolves,
brother nomads,
fellow pedestrians from the Pleistocene.

Chapter 7

A FLEETING GLIMPSE

To see a wolf in the wild has become a fond wish for millions. Most of us have seen numerous photographs, paintings or films, and we think we know exactly what the animal looks like. But a real live wolf remains but a dream, a ghost hidden in the shadows of forest, a phantom of the wintry wilds. At night we imagine that we hear its eerie howl. Or was it only the wind moaning in the spruce tops? And yet, often enough, in the bright light of day we come across its tracks, large and sprawling in mud or snow.

Accidental sightings, along roads and highways, seem to happen most often to people who are not particularly keen on wildlife. Such as the party of skiers, in a hurry to get to the slopes of Jasper, who almost ran into "a bunch of German shepherds" that seemed to be in hot pursuit of a deer or an elk.

Such luck seldom comes to naturalists or budding wildlife photographers who drive or walk the park's trails with wolves on their minds. And if the hoped-for encounter finally arrives, we seldom get more than a fleeting glimpse of a dog-like animal loping across our path. Was it really a wolf? What we see and what we remember depends on circumstance and may vary as much as the physical appearance of the wolf itself.

Wolves come in many colors, from coal-black to white, from reddish-brown to yellow-tan, and their color pattern varies from one animal to the next. Some have black heads and legs, with silver or copper-toned bodies. Others have white or grizzled faces with prominent black markings on head, rump or tail that set them apart from fellow members of the tribe. In size, wolves range from scarcely larger than a coyote to as tall and long-legged as a deer.

Based on differences in size, pelage color and skull characteristics between wolves collected in various parts of the continent, early taxonomists named 24 subspecies for North America alone. However, their sample of specimens was rather small. Recent work using both cranial measurements and molecular genetics suggests that only five subspecies are warranted. And even among those there is individual variation and overlap. The largest wolves, of which many are black, live in Alaska and western Canada. They can attain a weight of 40-55 kg (88-125 lbs), about a third heavier than the white arctic wolf and the gray wolf of eastern North America. The smallest subspecies are the Mexican wolf, now practically exterminated in the wild (but on its way back through reintroduction!) and the red wolf of the southwestern United States, which was saved from extinction by the skin of its teeth.

According to evolutionary theory, both the wolf and the hoofed mammals derived from a common ancestor that existed a hundred million years ago. Predator and prey evolved in association with each other, locked in an ever-lasting contest to improve physically and sharpen wits. While the prey became better adapted for the early detection of danger and a swift escape, the predator had to improve its aggressive capability to overcome the prey's increasingly effective defenses.

About fifty million years ago, the primitive ancestors of the wolf split into a variety of branches that culminated in the development of more specialized carnivores, including bears, weasels, raccoons, cats, foxes and the dog family, or *Canidae*. It is thought that the legendary dire wolf developed in South America. It later invaded the north and became quite common from coast to coast, sharing the continent with sabre-toothed

tigers, lions and mammoths. Hundreds of well-preserved skeletons of the great dire wolf have been found in the famous Rancho La Brea tar pits in California. This once so successful species became extinct during the last Pleistocene glaciation, some ten thousand years ago.

As determined by the study of fossils and genetic relationships, *Canis lupus* the modern-day wolf of America, Asia and Europe, is believed to have originated in North America from the coyote line about a million years ago. Ironically, the close relationship of the two, wolf and coyote, has given rise to some heated arguments about current efforts to reintroduce wolves to areas where they have been exterminated, particularly in the American southwest and southeast that used to be inhabited by the smallest subspecies of wolves.

In 1987, after the red wolf had been placed under the protection of the Endangered Species Act, fourteen of the last survivors were captured by the U.S. Fish and Wildlife Service and taken to special breeding facilities. They produced young in captivity and some of them, with their parents, have been released into wild habitats in North Carolina and Tennessee. This program of reintroduction has turned into a modern success story of wildlife management and recovery. However, the continuation of the program has recently run into opposition. New research by geneticists disclosed that the red wolf may not be a true wolf at all but a hybrid between gray wolves and coyotes. The evidence came to light after scientists compared mitochondrial DNA between red wolves, gray wolves and coyotes. They found genetic patterns in the red wolf of coyotes and gray wolves but none that was unique to the red wolf. If this small, rufous-colored southern wolf is indeed just a hybrid, some people argue, the costly breeding program should be discontinued because the Endangered Species Act does not protect hybrids.

In a formal announcement, made in December of 1991, the U.S. Fish and Wildlife Service proclaimed that the red wolf was not a hybrid. One of its scientists, professor Ronald Nowak, believes that the red wolf is indeed a valid species or at the very least a subspecies of the gray wolf. In fact, based on new analysis of fossils and modern specimens, Nowak theorizes that the red wolf is the forbearer of all wolves. Over aeons of evolutionary time, it spread across North America to Asia and Europe. During the glacial periods, when sea levels dropped and a land bridge formed between Alaska and Siberia, some of these Eurasian wolves returned to North America and gave rise to the present race of large wolves that inhabits the north. The current population of the red wolf may thus be a remnant of the original wolf. Nowak does not deny that there is hybridization between coyotes and wolves, but that does not necessarily mean that the red is a hybrid to begin with. And, stated the professor, current recovery efforts should be pursued vigorously.

Interbreeding of coyotes and wolves is also occurring in eastern Canada and the northeastern States, where resident wolves are 30-40 percent smaller than western wolves. The vast majority of eastern wolves look in fact much like coyotes with their gray-brown fur and rufous ears. Hybridization of coyotes and wolves, and perhaps with domestic dogs, has produced an eastern coyote that is bigger and heavier than its western kin. Locally called "brush wolves", they can surpass weights of 20 kg (44 lbs) and have become habitual predators of deer in parts of Quebec, Ontario, the Maritime provinces, as well as the eastern states.

The question that needs to be asked is this: If the smaller wolves and coyotes interbreed so readily, doesn't that indicate that they are one and the same species? Classically, a species is defined as a group of organisms capable of reproducing within itself but not with other groups. For instance, red foxes and coyotes cannot interbreed; they are not of the same genus and do not have the same number of chromosomes in their genetic make-up. By contrast, other members of the canid family, such as wolves, coyotes and domestic dogs, do have the same chromosome number and could therefore mate with each other, producing fertile offspring. However, dog/wolf or dog/coyote hybrids may have no future in the wild because their reproductive physiology is disrupted; dogs breed year-round, whereas wild canids are seasonal breeders.

Another valid question seems to be: is the coyote just a subspecies of its bigger cousin? Perhaps it is the other way round. As scientists tell us and as stated earlier in this chapter, the wolf evolved from the coyote line. Normally, species and subspecies are separated geographically which prevents interbreeding. However, when they become pushed together, perhaps as a result of shrinking habitats, the opportunity for mixing occurs. This was in fact the scenario in North America during the past century. And the catalyst for this change was the arrival in the New World of another species, even more adaptable than the canids, our own.

In the early days of human settlement, *Canis latrans* the coyote, was absent from most if not all of Canada and the eastern States. Its ancestral homelands were the arid prairies and deserts of the southwest. However, in this century, the adaptable coyote has expanded its range across the continent, all the way to Alaska and Yukon. Eastward, it advanced into the maritime provinces and the Atlantic states. Quite recently, it even managed to conquer Newfoundland by crossing the ice of Cabot Strait!

This continental window of opportunity for the coyote was opened up by the local disappearance of the competition. In the last century, human settlement and large-scale destruction of natural habitats were followed by the extirpation of wolves from most of the United States and southern Canada. It created vast new living space for the adaptable coyote. From coast to coast, the little interloper is now the principal representative of the wild canid family, as it may have been in the shadowy past before the wolf developed from its genes, and long before the first humans set foot on the continent.

Chapter 8

OF WOLVES AND HUMANS

It must have been a shaggy procession of people who followed the wolf trails that led from Asia onto the North American continent. It happened during one of the ice ages when a land bridge had formed across the Bering Strait. As the climate cooled, great amounts of sea water had been taken up by the polar icecap that expanded from the arctic and grew southward. It resulted in a steep drop in ocean levels that left the chain of islands that now lie between Siberia and Alaska high and dry. According to popular (but recently challenged) theory, the first humans arrived in America some ten to twenty thousand years ago during the last glaciation of the Pleistocene. The Eurasian wolf is believed to have entered via the same route but much earlier.

Like the wolves, the two-legged immigrants were experienced hunters who found their new home bountiful in prey species. In a relatively brief period, the nomads spread far south to central America and beyond. Perhaps they were forced to move fast, fleeing from other tribes that came after them. Bloody conflict, sparked by territorial competition, may have been as natural between bands of early humans as it is among wolf packs.

In terms of lifestyle there are several other customs which stone-age people had in common with wolves. Both kill large prey by cooperative methods. Both live in family groups, and males as well as females take part in caring for the young, quite in contrast to prey species such as deer and moose; their offspring is raised only by their mother. Early Inuit and Indians left no written record of their ancestral attitudes toward the powerful and dangerous carnivores which competed with them for certain prey species. We can only go by the testimony of the first white travelers who came to North America at a much later stage. Wherever the European scouts encountered aboriginal peoples, there were also many wolves. Apparently, the two nations, human and animal, lived side by side. There is little doubt that some occasional lethal conflict may have taken place. At other times, people may have profited from wild predators and utilized the remains of their kills. By and large, the Indian seems to have had no quarrel with the wolf and considered him a brother in the hunt. In the religious beliefs of many tribes, wolves as well as bears were honored and respected as kindred spirits.

How different was the attitude toward the wild dogs among the first white settlers! Since Grecian and Roman times, the wolf had been the scourge of pastoral man all across Europe and the Middle East. In early mythology and in the Bible, it was referred to as rapacious and bloodthirsty. It skulked through folklore and fables as the personification of evil and treachery. The superstition that people changed into werewolves at night, committing acts of unspeakable cruelty, became the basis for the witchcraft persecutions in the Middle Ages when suspected werewolves were burned at the stake by the Inquisition.

Coming from a culture where the hated beast had long been associated with the devil, the English pilgrims who settled the eastern shores of America began their war on wolves soon after they arrived. Deeply religious and God-fearing, they viewed themselves as sacrificial lambs and the wolf as the anti-Christ that had to be summarily exterminated from the "howling wilderness" of the New World.

In Britain it had been the task of mounted noblemen to rid the country of wolves. They were driven out of their lair with armies of beaters and pursued with hounds and mastiffs bred for the purpose. In Scotland and elsewhere, forests were set on fire to destroy the wolf's hideouts. In many parts of the European mainland, the species was not extirpated until the early 1900s, and it has managed to hang on until today across the east, south and north, from Greece to Portugal, from Italy to Sweden, with healthy populations in Spain, Poland and Russia. By contrast, partly because of the insular nature of their islands, the Anglo-Saxons were successful at exterminating the wolf at a very early date. The wild dogs vanished from England in the late 1400s, from Scotland and Ireland by the mid-1700s.

In America, the extermination of the wolf proved to be a formidable task which was seen as the major obstacle to the expansion of livestock raising. For several centuries, the wolf remained the most potent enemy threatening the precarious existence of immigrant peasants who wanted to replace the American wilderness with fields and pastures. Actual losses of domestic animals to predation were not heavy at first, even though early pioneers allowed their pigs, goats and sheep to roam at will over the clearings and adjacent woods. But problems began to grow worse after the wolf's natural prey, the hoofed animals, were hunted out. Many agreed with George Washington that the wolf could never be exterminated from the east and mid-west. How wrong he was! But it took three hundred years of persistent killing and millions of dollars in bounty payments.

The practice of rewarding those who killed wolves began in ancient Greece and has been more or less continuous in Europe for 2,700 years. The British colonists who came to New England were well-versed in the use and administration of bounty payments. They installed the first incentive for wolf killing in

1630, just ten years after the Mayflower landed at Plymouth. Bounty payments were not always in money. In Virginia, wolf killers were remunerated with tobacco which was in wide use as a currency for a century or more. Pennsylvania hired professional wolf hunters in 1705. Elsewhere, monetary rewards were often high enough to make the hunting of wolves worthwhile. Even the local Indians were offered money or goods to kill wolves. By the close of the 1700s, wolves had practically disappeared from most of New England, but remained in other eastern States, from Maine to Florida, until the 1900s.

The early methods of wolf destruction were legion and varied from the most primitive to the ingenious and from relatively humane to terribly cruel. Pitfalls, already used in antiquity by Egyptians and Romans, were the most common technique. It involved the digging of deep holes that were covered and concealed with a thin mat of branches and grass. They were located on wolf runways and baited with meat. The animal that fell into the pit was prevented from jumping out because the hole was widest at the bottom. Pointed sticks might be set into the floor and sides. In other regions, shepherds dug steep trenches around a staked live goat. The trench narrowed toward the bottom and was lined with slippery poles, tightly wedging the unfortunate creature that fell in.

Pitfalls were also in use by native North Americans. But more often the Indians constructed so-called corral traps of wooden poles set in a circle and leaning inwards. At one point, an earthen ramp allowed predators to enter, enticed by a bait, but they were prevented from jumping out by the angle of the poles. The most clever contraption devised by the Indians for capturing wild furbearers was the "falling trap" or deadfall. If an animal pulled at the bait, it dislodged a stake and triggered the fall of a heavy load of stones or logs that crushed the animal's spine, killing it at once. Some natives were very adept at setting spring-loaded snares on game trails to capture rabbits and the smaller predators. The snares were attached to a bent sapling which sprang back into position, lifting the animal high off the ground, as soon as the snare was pulled.

The cruellest device, employed by certain coastal tribes, was designed to let large carnivores hang themselves. It consisted of a ball of meat or fat in which a sharp fish hook was embedded. The ball was suspended from a tree, and the animal that jumped up and grabbed the bait in its mouth was condemned to an agonizing death. Inuit wolf hunters in the arctic employed an equally mean device: a sharply pointed whale baleen, coiled and bound with a sinew and frozen into a ball of tallow. If swallowed, the bait melted, the sinew dissolved and the uncoiling bone pierced the animal's stomach.

In addition to some of the ancient methods described above, the European settlers defended their livestock interests against the wolf with wire snares, set guns and crude metal gin traps. The modern Newhouse leghold trap, unchanged until today, was not invented until 1843.

Poison, by far the most destructive means of killing wild canids, was little used in colonial times. But when it finally proliferated, in the latter part of the 1800s, the wolf's fate, and that of many other carnivorous mammals and birds, was doomed, not only in the eastern United States, but right across the continent, from the Atlantic to the Pacific, and from the Gulf of Mexico to the 49th parallel which marks the border with Canada.

The earliest known toxic substance used in killing wild animals is a bitter drug called strychnine that acts by over-stimulation of the nervous system. When ingested in sufficient dosage, death comes quickly to any animal, including humans, preceded by violent trembling and convulsions. Strychnine is derived from the flat, round beans of a tree Strychnos nux-vomica that grows in India and Australia, also known by the common names of bachelor button, poison nut or vomiting bean. The poison comes in the form of a powder or crystals and can be mixed with water for easy preparation of grain or meat balls. Apparently, its toxic properties have been known for five centuries and it was utilized in England as early as the mid-1600s to destroy rats, dogs and crows. Today, strychnine is still sold in drug- and hardware stores to landowners in rural districts for the purpose of ridding fields and pastures of ground-squirrels and gophers. Unfortunately, the poison can be chain-reactive; scavengers, such as hawks, crows and gulls, may die too if they eat the entrails of poisoned rodents. Strychnine-treated grain distributed at random for gophers may be picked up by geese and ducks that have been known to fall dead out of the sky. Unauthorized use of strychnine by ranchers and hunters to destroy wild canids undoubtedly takes place too, but is hard to detect or stop.

In the early days, the use of poison to kill wolves began to grow to horrendous proportions after fur scouts and trappers ventured west, in the United States as well as in Canada. Unlike the pioneering settlers of the east, the explorers of the prairie were not simply intent on destroying "varmints" because they menaced domestic stock, but because of their pelts. Especially after beavers had been trapped out, wolf fur became quite valuable and it was easy to obtain. Instead of carrying heavy traps, all a "wolfer" needed were a few bottles of strychnine. He shot a bison for bait, cut the meat into small cubes, and inserted a quantity of crystals into each. After scattering the morsels about the carcass, the wolfer simply waited for the results. In this way, tens of thousands, perhaps hundreds of thousands of wild canids were destroyed all across the west.

In the late 1800s, when the prairie was stocked with cattle, the major players in the war on wolves changed again. Now it was primarily the cowboy who sought the destruction of the remaining packs. After their natural prey, the bison, became extinct, the "buffalo wolves" were forced to kill domestic animals. There is much documented evidence that the last of the lobos did a number on the dimwitted cattle that grazed the open range.

Often, only the choicest parts of a cow or steer were eaten and the predators seldom returned to the kill. The wolves learned to be cautious and some became uncannily smart at avoiding traps and poisons. The cowboy's vengeance and hatred increased. As pointed out by Stanley Young, it is a psychological twist typical of western cattlemen that they could be very pragmatic and even philosophical in the face of severe livestock losses inflicted on them by drought, disease or winter starvation. But let a thief take one of their flock and they were ready to lynch the culprit, be it man or beast.

To rid the range of the "curse of wolves" American farm associations as well as state and country offices began to offer hefty bounties and free strychnine to anyone who wanted to kill them. It was an unwritten law of the West that any stockman who found a steer or heifer dead on the range, sprinkled the carcass with a liberal dose of strychnine. This callous practice not only led to the destruction of countless wolves, but also eagles, ravens and all kinds of smaller predators and scavengers. It is a miracle that some of these species survived this destructive period in the history of the United States.

Theodore Roosevelt, who later became president and designated Yellowstone as the world's first national park, was one of the most outspoken westerners who agitated for federal action to exterminate "the beast of waste and desolation." In 1915, Congress appropriated funds for the hiring of federal agents to control predators. It stopped the indiscriminate poisoning and eventually led to the suspension of the often fraudulent bounties in most of the western states. It also brought the war on wolves close to its bitter end.

Stanley Young was among the specialists who were hired as federal wolf hunters. He later published a classic book called *The Wolves Of North America* co-authored with Edward Goldman. Young also wrote *The Last Of The Loners* which describes in vivid detail his exploits in hunting down some of the most notorious cattle killers, such as the white Custer wolf that eluded hundreds of men with guns, traps and poison for six years. Perhaps characteristic of these men, and typical of the paradox of the hunter, Young never seemed to have hated the wolf, instead he expressed respect and even admiration for the animal he so ardently sought to outwit and destroy. He wrote: "Where not in conflict with human interests, wolves may well be left alone. They form one of the most interesting groups of mammals and should be permitted to have a place in the North American fauna."

America's violent relationship with the wolf continues until today although there have been great improvements. Outside Alaska, the species survived in the northeast. There are now more than 2,000 wolves in Minnesota and they are expanding into neighboring states. A phenomenon of the last decade is their return to the West. Dispersing south from Canada, packs have established a home on the range from Montana to Wyoming. In 1995 wolves captured in Canada were released in Yellowstone and Idaho, where they are now breeding and increasing. Plans exist also to reintroduce them to various regions in the southwest and the east. Wherever it returns, the wild dog becomes controversial and there are still many people who think that the only good wolf is a dead one.

However, in the mind of the general public its image has changed profoundly, from the devil incarnate to a respected member of our wild heritage. To an increasing majority of American city-dwellers, the wolf is now almost as beloved as Bambi. In rural areas of the wolf's current range, man the hunter and man the shepherd still may have some trouble to share the land with this formidable competitor, but by and large the species' future seems assured. The American war on wolves has finally come to an end.

Chapter 9

A PRICE ON HIS HEAD

Imagine their consternation when the first Francophone settlers set eyes on their adopted homeland in eastern Canada. The year was 1608, soon after the French explorers Jacques Cartier and Samuel de Champlain placed their country's tricolor on the present sites of Quebec and Montreal. To the immigrant peasants, accustomed to the picturesque scenery of pastoral Europe, the rocky bays of the great St. Lawrence River must have looked cold and forbidding. On the shore stood a brooding wall of boreal forest, covering the country like an evergreen mantle from Labrador to the Pacific. Around all early farming communities of "New France", particularly after night closed in, the howl of wolves must have been a common sound.

Yet, the "Canadiens" proved to be a hardy and adaptable lot, and they may have been more tolerant of wolves than the British colonists south of the border. Sure, near the homestead, wolves could be a menace to the peasant's very existence. It must have been a terrible discovery to find your only goat or cow dead or wounded in the morning. But the presence of wolves in the backcountry may have been considered quite acceptable. It might

To hear wolf song in the wilderness has become a fond wish for many. When you can actually see the animal that is howling, its call may seem to come from much farther away. Could this be a ventriloquistic ruse so as not to unduly alarm prey? Wolves certainly do not howl to scare other animals. Distant howls are usually ignored by deer, elk or sheep. However, a howl at close range will make them look up warily into the direction of the sound.   *Photos: Monte Sloan, Wolf Park.*

In deep snow, wolf packs often travel single-file, stepping exactly in each other's footprints to save energy. If the trail splits, it is possible to tell how many wolves passed by. In this photo, a pack of seven traversed a muskeg where snow was nearly 1 meter (3 feet) deep. *Photo: Dick Dekker.*

Wolves are excellent swimmers and not afraid to cross the swiftest of rivers. During winter, ice facilitates their travels but there is a risk of falling through. Experienced wolves are careful when crossing ice; they can probably detect thin spots through their foot soles or by listening to water gurgling below the surface.

Photo: Monte Sloan, Wolf Park.

During the bitter cold of early winter, a great elk bull, attacked by wolves, took refuge in an open stretch of a swift river in Jasper National Park. Bleeding from wounds in the rump and already weakened by the demands of the fall rutting season, the bull eventually succumbed and froze into the ice. In March, after the carcass began thawing out, the pack returned. Between meals, wolves lie up some distance away, tucking their nose under the tail.

Photos: (top) Dick Dekker, (bottom) Monte Sloan, Wolf Park.

100

During 1983-1985, Alberta provincial biologists studied the food habits of the Brazeau wolf pack that denned inside Jasper National Park but ranged far across the boundaries. For two months each winter, the radio-collared pack of ten to fourteen animals was tracked daily by helicopter. It killed prey, varying from deer to wild horses, every 2.6 days on average. The photo shows two members of the pack near the remains of a moose calf. Also the cow was killed. Predation rates in Yellowstone were reported to be much higher. Some small packs pulled down an elk each day. Similar surplus killing was reported from Banff National Park during the 1980s in the early years after the wolves' return there, when elk were numerous and lacked experience in avoiding wolf attack.

Photo: Ken Schmidt, Alberta Fish and Wildlife.

Ever-ready to defend itself with sharp hooves, an adult moose has little to fear from wolves unless it is weakened by starvation or disease. However, by killing young calves, predators such as wolves and bears can keep moose densities down across the northwoods to less than 50 per 100 km² (38 square miles). If heavy hunting by humans is superimposed on natural predation, moose densities drop even further and often give rise to demands from northern residents for wolf control. *Photo: Tom Branch.*

The daily routine of all prey species is governed by the twin necessities of eating and not being eaten. To lessen the risk of wolf predation, tundra caribou band together, travel all the time and forage on the run. But the woodland caribou (in the picture) is a recluse that keeps its movements to a minimum, particularly in winter, leaving few tracks that could betray its presence. *Photo: Tom Branch.*

Elk attempt to avoid wolves and bears in a number of ways. In Jasper Park, elk cows with calves are common along roads and in camp-grounds where grazing is good and large predators are scarce. In Banff National Park, after wolves became common during the 1980s, elk increased in the townsite, creating numerous problems. (Even road signs had to be placed for them! HaHaHa...!)

Photos: Dick Dekker.

In defense, deer have been known to gore wolves with their sharp antlers, or even to kill them with one well-placed kick to the head. However, by and large, this graceful denizen of the woods rather flees than fights. In the western mountains, the mule deer relies on its sensitive hearing for early warning. To get away it has plenty of speed and agility, as well as an intimate knowledge of the terrain. Bounding in a high, stiff-legged gait, it escapes easily unless it stumbles, runs into an ambush or is tired out after dogged pursuit. *Photo: Dick Dekker.*

During summer, Rocky Mountain bighorns disperse widely over steep alpine slopes where predators are scarce. When snow comes, they concentrate on winter ranges at lower elevations. To lessen the risk of wolf attack, the sure-footed sheep stay close to cliffs. However, if the steeper terrain becomes overgrazed, hunger will force them out into less secure habitat. *Photo: Dick Dekker.*

This rare shot of a lone wolf chasing mountain sheep was taken from the Maligne Road in Jasper National Park in October 1990. The lamb made a narrow escape down the rocky slope while the wolf fell down some distance but did not seem to be hurt.   *Photo copyright © Hughson, Trottier, Schelhas.*

Young wolf pups have chubby baby-faces, but at three months, ears and feet look awkwardly oversized. Black puppies often have a white spot on the chest that usually disappears later on. Rare in eastern North America, black-phase wolves are common in the West, making up about one third of the population. In Jasper National Park, during the early 1990s, the proportion increased from 50 to about 90 percent. With age, the face or legs of dark animals may turn silvery-white, and some black wolves have been known to become entirely bluish-gray in one or two years. *Photos: Monte Sloan, Wolf Park.*

The reintroduction of wolves to Yellowstone National Park has been a tremendous success, both for the animals and the many people who supported the program from the beginning. The photo shows Yellowstone biologists Douglas Smith and Michael Phillips carrying a sedated wolf. New arrivals, captured in Canada, were retained in holding pens for ten weeks prior to release. This acclimation period is credited in part for the program's success. Upon release, the wolves stayed near where they were put and did not head back to Canada, as many critics had predicted. Another important measure of success is the fact that the adaptable animals have reproduced from their first year onward. Moreover, there has been very little predation on livestock in areas bordering the park. Studies of the ecological impact of the wolves in Yellowstone are ongoing. During winter they prey mostly on older elk, averaging 14 years of age. The wolves also kill coyotes, which used to be abundant in the park and virtually eliminated reproduction in pronghorn antelopes by killing fawns. "Whatever the wolves do to reshape Yellowstone, their return is good," writes Doug Smith. "We owe a thanks to Canadians for not letting their wolves go the way the Yellowstone wolf did earlier this century. Our job now is to ensure that what we did before never happens again." *Photo: Call of the Wild Photography, NPS.*

Wolf specialists from across the USA cooperated in a smoothly orchestrated campaign beginning with the capture of wolves in Alberta in 1995, and terminating in their successful release in Yellowstone and Idaho. The top photo depicts a scene from the foothills near Jasper National Park. Darted from a helicopter, a sedated wolf is prepared for transport to headquarters by Alaskan Ken Taylor. The lower photograph shows the application of a radio-collar by Yellowstone veterinarian Mark Johnson and Isle Royale wolf biologist Rolf Peterson.

Photos: (top) LuRay Parker/WG&F, USF&WS; (bottom) Jim Peaco, NPS.

Wolf number ten, a splendid big male, was captured near Jasper, Alberta, in January of 1995. The lower photo features him in a holding case, ready for transit to Yellowstone. Number ten was reintroduced to wolf #9, his prospective mate, in the Rose Creek acclimation pen where the pair stayed for ten weeks. After release, the female gave birth to eight pups, unfortunately just outside the park and #10 was illegally shot. However, his genes will live on. His black mate became the heroine of Yellowstone. She soon paired up with another male and not only raised her eight pups, but produced litters of three and six in the next two years. In 1997, after a severe winter, Yellowstone wolf numbers surged; several of the eight packs in the park produced more than one litter of pups.

Photo: (top) Call of the Wild Photography, NPS; (bottom) LuRay Parker/ WG&F, USF&WS.

The Mexican wolf, a smallish race of the gray wolf, was extirpated in the wild only decades ago. Fortunately, the very last survivors were taken into captivity. By 1996, through the dedicated efforts of 29 breeding facilities in the USA and Mexico, the animals had multiplied to 150. The following year, plans were approved to release ten or more family groups into the Blue Range Wolf Recovery Area straddling New Mexico and Arizona. The photo was taken at a desert breeding facility. The "lobo" has shorter fur and relatively larger ears than its northern relatives. *Photo: Monte Sloan.*

explain why the first wolf bounties in eastern Canada were not instituted until 1793, more than 160 years later than in New England.

The French Canadians included many colorful individuals who mixed easily with the natives, often intermarrying, and who began a lively trade in animal skins. The cold northern climate produced a superior quality of fur that brought high prices on the fashion markets of Paris. Guided by Indians, the voyageurs and half-breeds penetrated the interior of the continent in search of rich new trapping grounds. Recognizing a profitable deal when they saw one, the British, never far behind, formed the famous Hudson's Bay Company, an enterprise of "Gentlemen Adventurers Trading into Hudson's Bay". It received royal charter from King Charles II and a virtual monopoly to do business in the vast territory drained by rivers flowing into the Hudson's Bay.

Competition between French and British fur companies was the catalyst that spurred them on in exploration of the western hinterland, well ahead of developments on the American side of the border. Canadian scouts made epic journeys up the great rivers to the Rocky Mountains sixty years before the Lewis and Clark expedition reached Montana. One of the earliest Hudson's Bay scouts, a Scotsman named Anthony Hendry (later spelled Henday), travelled west by canoe and by horse as far as present day Alberta in 1754. His diaries paint a fascinating picture of wildlife on the virgin prairie. He reported seeing elk, moose and multitudes of bison. Shadowing the shaggy herds were many wolves. "At times, it was difficult to say which were more numerous, them or the buffalo."

Hendry's mission was to establish direct contact with the Blackfoot Indians, the horse-mounted warriors of the plains. In central Alberta, on the banks of the South Saskatchewan River, he was cordially welcomed in a large camp containing more than a thousand teepees. Hendry presented the elders with metal axes, cooking pots and trinkets. He then made his spiel, urging the Blackfoot to bring their furs to the Company fort on the shores of the Hudson's Bay (instead of bartering them to the Montreal traders!).

The chiefs replied: "Why should our young men embark on a long, hazardous journey to your post, when all we need in life is right here?" Hendry had to admit that the rolling prairie, studded with lakes and woods, and home to abundant wildlife, looked indeed like a paradise.

But the good life of the Indians proved to be fragile. Beside many useful goods, the Europeans brought diseases, such as smallpox, that wiped out three-quarters of western Indians in the next century. The Indians were also at war between themselves. White settlement in Ontario forced the displacement of eastern tribes that ventured west to conquer new territory. Armed with rifles, they battled the plains Indians and inflicted heavy carnage on the wildlife resources, not only on the furbearers but also on the hoofed mammals. By the late 1800s, even before the new railroad brought growing numbers of settlers and sodbusters, the destruction intensified. The once so numerous bison were exterminated, the woods burned, the prairie broken, and the proud Indian became a pauper in his former paradise.

What about the buffalo wolves? They vanished with their dwindling prey, never to return, even before the demise of the wolves in the western United States. The reason had to do with the fur trade, which opened up the Canadian West at a relatively early time. Shooting and trapping of wolves was common practice. And in 1859, Hudson's Bay postmasters were already placing strychnine baits in the mountains of present-day Jasper National Park. But a major factor that sealed the wolf's final doom was the disappearance of its prey. Bands of trappers, Indians as well as whites and halfbreeds, explored all of the foothills and mountains, living largely off the land. The late 1800s were also marked by a series of extremely cold winters. The combination of deep snow and overhunting led to the near extermination of all hoofed mammals in western Alberta by the end of the 1800s.

It was not until the beginning of the new century that the idea of conservation began to take hold. Game laws were passed that regulated shooting seasons, ended market hunting and limited the number of animals that licensed individuals could kill. It was a revolutionary measure that brought slow dividends. Fortunately, environmental conditions for a return of hoofed mammals were favorable. There was an abundance of food. Large-scale fires, often deliberately set to create grassland, had replaced the old-growth forest with young stands that contained abundant browse. Moreover, at least initially, there was a scarcity of predators.

During the 1930s, moose, elk, deer, and bighorn sheep began to multiply to greater densities than ever before. Eventually, also the wolves came back. They returned to all of the mountains of western Canada and became common in the forested portions of the prairie provinces as well as in Ontario and Quebec. In settled regions where the species ran into opposition from farmers and hunters, old fears and economic conflict flared up again and sparked a return to bounty payments.

However, an important question that was beginning to be asked was this: How effective were the bounties in reducing the incidence of wolf predation on livestock? From the viewpoint of the wildlife manager, support for bounties was not universal. For one thing, they were costly. Over a million dollars was spent each in Ontario and British Columbia during the first half of the 1900s. Secondly, there was the possibility of fraud; there was no guarantee that dead wolves submitted for payment had actually been taken in the province which offered the incentive. And thirdly, over the long term, bounties did not appear to be effective in reducing wolf populations where and when needed.

One of the most prominent critics was Douglas Pimlott, a professor at the University of Toronto, who raised the issue at the first Canadian Predator Control Conference, held in 1954. After lively debate, a resolution was passed recommending that all provinces consider the possibility of simultaneously abandoning the bounty system. The western provinces complied with it very soon, while Ontario and Quebec held out for some time. In fact, the ancient idea of paying citizens for the killing of wolves is still not quite dead. In the 1990s, some eastern municipalities and townships have in fact reinstated bounty payments on a local scale, albeit temporarily and even illegally.

The irony of Pimlott's successful crusade was that he soon found out that the bounty system was "not necessarily the greatest evil" and that its replacement constituted "a greater abuse and a greater waste of public funds." The replacement, which had been recommended by Pimlott and others, was wolf control by government agents, but only where and when needed. Unfortunately, it became a method of where and when *wanted* by special interest groups such as hunters and stock breeders. The new system had other alarming aspects and the costs soon exceeded all bounty payments.

In 1961, Pimlott wrote an article for *Canadian Audubon* which he began with the following, now famous, challenge: "The wolf poses one of the most important conservation questions of our time. Will the species still exist when the twentieth century passes into history? Or will man have exterminated the wolf as a final demonstration of his "conquest" of the wilderness and of wild things that dare to compete and conflict with him?"

It took another quarter century of conflict and debate between wolf killers and wolf defenders before Pimlott's fears could be allayed and before the outlook on the future of Canada's wolves began to brighten.

Chapter 10

IF A RAVEN FALLS

The vast lonely land that is Canada's North lies under a shroud of snow, as if to cover its dead. There is no color other than the sombre green of spruce and the gray of wind-blown rock. Higher ridges are veiled by ice fog, rising on a ceaseless draft into the frigid air. The sky is a pale blue void that has sucked the last breath of warmth out of the dormant wilderness. There is no sound. Silence is total except one's own breathing and the urgent hiss of blood pressure in the inner ear.

But wait... Isn't that an aircraft, too far to be seen? The faint throb of an engine increases in volume, and a distant speck grows in substance and shape. A silver Cessna banks low over a frozen lake. It circles once and drops an object that hits the snow-covered surface in a puff of powder. The aircraft's engine roars and the machine pulls up at speed, disappearing into the distance. The sound dies to a spasmodic sobbing until the silence is again complete.

Wait again... Was that the croak of a raven? Searching the fathomless sky, the eye focuses with ecstasy on the black bird, sentinel of the empty land, companion of the wolf! His wingbeats rasp loudly on the still air. His display of vitality defies the cold and restores one's confidence in the living. His guttural voice is content, exuding well-being like the purring of a warm cat. He has seen the odd object on the lake. He knows it is food, the hind quarters of a hoofed animal. The bird circles and descends on the snow with a hop and a skip. Warily, he flicks his wingtips and waits until his mate arrives. They encourage each other to approach the bait. Before the end of the short winter day, the black birds will fly to their roost with full crops.

If a poisoned raven drops off its branch during the night, will it matter to anyone? If a tree falls in the wilderness will there be a crash if there is no-one to hear it? Will the lighting be followed by thunder if there is no human ear to register the tearing of sky over the lonely land?

After the bounty system was abandoned, the first Canadian province to employ special government agents for the killing of wolves was British Columbia. In 1947, it formed a predator control division with twelve permanent staff members. The tool of choice was poison. In addition to the conventional toxins, such as strychnine and cyanide, there was now a new substance, developed during the second world war, that was considered to be even more effective: compound 1080 (called "ten-eighty" or sodium monofluoro-acetate). It affected the nervous system, over-stimulating it until paralysis set in. The factors favoring its use were blandness and lack of odor. Its high solubility in water made application very easy; large baits could be injected with the fluid, rendering each portion of the meat toxic. In most jurisdictions, baits were placed and monitored with care. In others it was deemed convenient and cheap to drop them from the air, usually on frozen lakes. They were seldom retrieved in spring. After break-up, the left-overs sank to the bottom and were thought to be harmless.

In their defense, predator managers said that ten-eighty was "target-specific" and relatively more toxic for canids than for other scavengers such as birds which had to ingest quite a bit before the effect was lethal. The poison's negative side was that it was slow-acting; before dying, animals had time to disperse, making it difficult or impossible to check on results.

With minor variations, British Columbia's example was followed by other provinces, which used regular forestry and wildlife personnel or hired private trappers to do their wolf control. Aircraft were chartered to distribute baits across the wilderness.

During 1955-1960, Saskatchewan and Manitoba placed up to 340 baits per winter, the Northwest Territories 560, and British Columbia 2,100! The most startling figures are available from Alberta, which unleashed the fiercest poison campaign ever to be

conducted in Canada, or perhaps anywhere in the world. The stated reason was that rabies had reared its ugly head in the North. To prevent the southward spread of the feared disease, the province had made up its mind to exterminate all wild canids near settled areas. In 1952-1955, the following amounts of poison were distributed free to landowners and trappers: 106,100 cyanide cartridges and 628,000 strychnine pellets. In addition, the number of ten-eighty bait stations increased to 800 in 1956.

Up to this day, some biologists in the Alberta wildlife department believe that the action was justified. The mildest criticism is that the four-year campaign lasted too long and that the chief carriers of rabies were not only wild canids but also bats. Perhaps some wildlife officers saw the rabies-scare as a convenient excuse to once and for all rid the land of the hated wolf. To that end the campaign was a resounding success. The total kill was estimated at 5,200 wolves, as well as 171,000 coyotes and 55,000 foxes.

There were few estimates for other species, such as martens, cougars, bears and eagles. Their deaths were unavoidable. Hundreds, perhaps thousands, succumbed unnoticed and unnecessarily, their bones left to bleach in the wilderness. Foxes, wolverines and ravens became scarce over vast regions where they had been common before. Wolves were wiped out in all of the southern foothills and mountains, including the National Parks of Banff and Jasper. It was without a doubt one of the most shocking episodes in the continent-wide war on wolves.

The question of who had actually been responsible for starting the indiscriminate poisoning campaigns remains valid today. Who had ordered and supported the dastardly aerial missions over the western wilderness of Yukon and British Columbia? Who supervised the placing of poison baits on frozen lakes in Saskatchewan and Alberta, including Wood Buffalo National Park? There is no public record of the discussions that went on behind the scenes between provincial and federal wildlife directors. At that time, the general public did not seem to be overly concerned about the issue. But the insiders backing the campaigns, or actually involved in them, included some top-level biologists who believed in what they were doing and were well respected in their field.

Even Douglas Pimlott considered the aerial distribution of poison baits in the Northwest Territories a "valid approach to wildlife management" deemed necessary by the decline of barren-ground caribou which were believed to be in danger of extinction at that time. However, he *did* question the need for wolf control in regions of British Columbia where moose were already too numerous and starving, due to overpopulation on winter range. As he wrote in *Canadian Audubon*, Pimlott believed in control where and where *needed*, not where *wanted* by local interest groups such as hunters and ranchers.

In addition to his criticism of the unnecessary campaigns in British Columbia, Pimlott lamented the fact that provinces which were gung-ho on wolf control had failed to initiate a single research program. And it was from research that the final impetus to halt the poison campaigns was to come.

Alberta toned down its all-out campaign after 1956, but routine wolf poisoning on game ranges north and east of the National Parks continued until 1966. In other provinces and territories it took a few years longer before it was safe again for ravens to fly their ancient routes over the vast lonely land where so many had fallen...

Chapter 11

LET IT BE

In the much-quoted phrase of Aldo Leopold, only a mountain has lived long enough to listen objectively to the howl of a wolf. This metaphor may have been aimed particularly at Leopold's own profession of wildlife management, for it is certainly not true that a mountain, if it were capable of such thoughts, could afford to be objective. It simply had too much at stake. Elsewhere in his famous essay *Thinking like a mountain* Leopold admits that "just as a deer herd lives in mortal fear of its wolves, so does a mountain live in mortal fear of its deer."

In the absence of wolves, an overpopulation of deer can do irreparable harm to a mountain side, destroying trees and damaging the sod until it is eroded by run-off and blown to dust in the wind. There are numerous examples, in North America as well as the Old World, where this was allowed to happen, where grazing animals impoverished ecosystems that included not just wolves and deer but countless other wild creatures that depend on a well-balanced habitat for their existence.

Organizations of hunters and ranchers with a vested interest in favor of deer and against wolves have had their way for a very long time and resisted the change to a more objective view. Even Adolph Murie and Ian McTaggart-Cowan, the two prominent biologists who had done the first field studies on wolves in Alaska and Canada, had difficulty admitting to the new understanding. Despite the favorable things they had to say about wolves at the conclusion of their research in Denali and Jasper, both gentlemen recommended to their superiors that limited control should be continued in the parks. It was a recommendation they lived to regret. For the change to a more tolerant attitude toward predators was definitely in the wind, and like all ideas whose time has finally come, it proved unstoppable.

The turn-around in official thinking on wolf control was influenced by the publications of another pioneering field biologist, Paul Errington, whose work did not focus primarily on large mammal systems but on muskrats and quail, foxes and hawks. After exhaustive field observations, Errington concluded that the size of their populations was determined by ecological factors such as food and shelter, not by predation. However, if the number of muskrats or quail became too large for the available habitat, the foxes and hawks began to take a heavy toll of the "surplus" population, of individuals that had been forced to live in a poor environment and therefore had become vulnerable. By contrast, prey species in good habitat were quite sheltered from their enemies.

Errington's theory became the key argument in the emergence of a new philosophy of predator management in North America. However, the old ideas about wolf control died hard and actual policy did not begin to change until another force came into play, the general public.

One of the first popular wildlife books that portrayed the wolf in a favorable light was *Arctic Wild*, published in 1958. Its author, Lois Crysler, was not a professional biologist. She had assisted her husband in making a nature film on Alaska for Walt Disney Studios. During their long stay on the tundra, the couple had actually witnessed a number of incidents of wolves hunting caribou. Many were chased but those that were captured and killed proved to be debilitated by lung parasites or jaw bone disease. Like Murie, Crysler claimed that the effect of wolf predation on the caribou was actually a beneficial one. The sick and infirm were the first to be weeded out, while the healthy and strong were left to multiply their kind.

Another popular book that played a major role in reshaping the wolf's public image was *Never Cry Wolf* by the famous Canadian author Farley Mowat. First published in 1963, the best-seller was translated into many languages and made into a hilarious film, based on a potent mixture of fact, fiction and humor. In his youth, Mowat had been an assistant to a government biologist sent North to investigate the alarming decline of the barren-ground caribou. Mowat believed that the wolf had been made into a scapegoat, to be poisoned and shot everywhere, while the real culprit was man himself. During winter, parties of hunters came north in ski-equipped aircraft that could land on frozen lakes. Caribou habitually rest on lakes where they feel safe from ambush by wolves. However, there was no safety from the airborne hunters. They left the snow littered with carcasses and red with blood. Sometimes only the largest antlers and the choicest meat had been removed. People who came across these sites afterwards, falsely accused (the scavenging) wolves of the slaughter.

Mowat's clever and humorous narrative convinced masses of readers of the wolf's new image. The portrait he painted was that of a playful wild dog, a devoted parent to its family. During summer, it lived chiefly on mice, or so he claimed. His former colleagues accused Mowat of misrepresenting the facts, of stealing information from other biologists and advancing it as his own. But by and large, Mowat's message had the irresistible ring of truth; wolves were definitely not the major cause of the caribou declines. The gist of the message was underlined a few years later by Canadian caribou biologist J. F. Kelsall. His detailed monograph *The Migratory Caribou of Canada's North* included a scathing condemnation of the greed and irresponsibility of native and white trappers, who indulged in excessive killing of caribou for their own use and as food for their sledge dogs. Kelsall documented several extreme cases of waste and destruction in which Indians and Inuit shot hundreds of caribou just to cut out a few delicacies, such as the tongues or the unborn calves.

As the combined pressure from biologists and the general public began to mount, government agencies were forced to react. Caribou hunting regulations were tightened up and predator control programs were reviewed. During the same time, in the 1960s, all hoofed animals across the North had noticeably increased in number, partly in response to mild winters and to the decade-long poisoning of large predators. Abundant game populations, coupled with the changing attitudes about the role of predation, eventually led to a suspension of government wolf control in all provinces and territories, at least for a few years....until the pendulum of expert opinion swung back again.

Chapter 12

THE SILENCE IS BROKEN

Shattering the silence of wilderness, a helicopter descends over the canopy of forest, snow swirling off bending spruce tops. Below, six animals burst out of their beds in a panic. They are wolves, desperate to get away, bounding through deep snow between the trees. The machine banks in pursuit. Windows slide open and the barrels of shotguns are poked out. One after the other, five of the six collapse and crumple, their legs kicking spasmodically until all movement dies. The helicopter circles back, rotors clattering, and hovers over a thicket of trees, swaying in the draft. A small black pup of the year bolts from cover and races out into the open. The gun barrels buck twice, their report inaudible in the ear-splitting roar of engines. The wolf suddenly falls over, shuddering, at the end of a trail of red on white.

Who are these dastardly people? Poachers? Criminals? Neither. They are biologists, soberly doing their job at the direction of local government. They are the executioners with a new arm of their Wildlife Department charged with predator control. And the scene could have been set anywhere in northern Yukon, British Columbia or Alaska during the early 1980s.

What was the justification for this cold-blooded killing, this mafia-style method of terminating life? Doesn't the pursuit of animals by means of aircraft, giving them no chance of escape, harassing them until exhausted, go against our civilized principles of fair chase?

In their defense, biologists argue that aerial shooting is highly target-specific and selective. And it very seldom results in cripples as is the case in other methods of wolf control such as trapping. When caught in the steel jaws of a trap, wolves sometimes break away with an injured foot or even by dragging the cruel device along, maybe for weeks, until the animal dies of infection or starvation. By comparison, death by helicopter firing squad comes quickly, and biologists know exactly how many wolves are killed and where. From an ecological point of view, aerial shooting certainly seems preferable to the use of poison, which is by far the easiest and cheapest form of wolf control. By comparison, helicopter rental is expensive, amounting to about $1,500-2,600 per wolf shot! During the 1980s, in Alaska, Yukon and British Columbia, total expenditures for the "removal" of several thousand wolves ran into the millions of dollars. But the price to the public relations image of wildlife managers was high too. In the perception of many Canadians, Americans and Europeans, the airborne wolf killers ended up giving their profession a black eye.

Why was it necessary to control wolves anyway? Had not the biologists themselves, as recently as the early 1970s, spread the gospel of tolerance for predators? Wolves, they said, were not the major factor limiting prey populations. Scientific studies had proved repeatedly that the predators preyed mainly on the old, the very young and infirm. Wolf predation, many biologists believed, was compensatory; prey animals killed by wolves would have died of other causes anyway, such as disease or starvation, in the absence of predation. As a consequence of these new theories, wolf control had been abandoned in the late 1960s and 1970s. Why then had the clock been turned back again so soon? The explanation was simple but in need of some perspective.

After the poisoning campaigns of the previous two decades had been terminated, wolves quickly began to recover from their devastation all across the northwest. At that time, populations of hoofed mammals were very high, partly in response to better management of hunting. A series of mild winters had allowed maximum reproduction, coupled with the man-made scarcity of predators. The northwoods teemed with moose, caribou, elk and deer. Wolves, finally free from the scourge of poison, found their table set to overflowing. Family packs grew in size and wolf range expanded into areas where the species had not been seen for decades. But few people complained; there seemed plenty of venison to go around for everybody, hunters as well as predators.

Then, a disastrous scenario began to unfold very quickly. Locally, high concentrations of hoofed mammals caused overgrazing of winter range. Lack of food combined with deep snow are especially lethal for grazing animals such as elk. The winters of the late sixties and early seventies included some of the severest on record. Many elk and deer starved or failed to give birth to healthy calves the next year. It was nature's own drastic way of reducing the overpopulation of hoofed mammals. Added to that was excessive hunting pressure. Quotas were high and seasons long, lasting from September to January. In those days there were no restrictions on the number of female elk and moose that could be taken. During the same time, hunter access in the woods and mountains greatly expanded as a side effect of the booming development of natural resources. Oil and mining roads were bulldozed deep into former wilderness. Hunter mobility became unprecedented after the invention of snowmobiles and all-terrain vehicles. In many areas, humans began to kill a greater percentage of game animals, exceeding 10 or even 20 percent of the local population, than the species could afford to lose. Superimposed on the above climatic and man-made factors were the swelling numbers of predators, not only wolves but also cougars and bears. They were taking their toll of the declining prey base already weakened by severe winters and poor range. The combined impact of all detrimental factors became quite suddenly obvious at the end of the 1970s. Prey populations simply collapsed. Elk and caribou herds dwindled, moose and deer became scarce and hard to find. Guess who got the blame...? Yes, indeed, more and more hunters, laypeople as well as biologists, began to point their finger again at the big, bad wolf.

Rightly or wrongly, by the end of the seventies, increased pressure from hunting groups "to do something about the wolf problem" forced wildlife managers to again look at predator control as one of the first strategies aimed at bringing back the hoofed mammals. At that time, the use of poison had been ruled out. The only viable option seemed aerial shooting. Wolf hunting by aircraft had already been in vogue for some time in Alaska, particularly for private citizens. There, the move to government wolf hunting by aircraft seemed quite acceptable and caused few ripples of opposition. In the open tundra of Alaska it was easy to spot wolves from the air and to hit them with shotguns from small fixed-wing planes. However, in the wooded terrain of the Canadian Rocky Mountains and northern British Columbia, wolves often stayed in tree cover, making a clean shot chancy at best. So, the machine of choice for wolf managers in Canada became the helicopter. It was expensive but effective. Sure, aerial hunting of wolves was callous and unsporting. Not a single biologist professed to enjoy the job. But few outsiders knew about it and fewer protested. Local hunters, guide-outfitters and trappers, who were aware of what was going on in their backwoods, either applauded or said little against the practice, which they saw as the lesser of two evils. Until another player entered the picture, the general public....

The first whistle-blower who exposed the aerial wolf hunts in Canada to the news media was the Victoria-based anti-trapping group, the Association for the Protection of Fur-bearing Animals. One of its members had written to the government to protest against the aerial killing of wolves in the northeast of British Columbia, and she had received a letter from the provincial Environment Minister, Tony Brummet. He defended his Department's predator controls with the following statement: "Wolves may be pretty in a book or a contrived movie. In the bush under real conditions, they are one of the most vicious, wasteful and unrelenting killers in existence. Contrary to the Farley Mowat version, they do not selectively kill. A pack of wolves will kill as many animals in a herd as they can, often tearing them open and leaving them to die slowly."

The letter was released to the media and infuriated conservationists across the province and as far away as Ontario. Local papers carried dozens of letters from people opposed to the hunt. Some journalists ferried out details that embarrassed the politicians and further enraged the opposition. Apparently, in addition to $25,000 of government funds, the wolf-kill was financed by hunter groups and the Northern Guides Association which had organized a $100,000 raffle. But most of the initial cost of the program, estimated at a quarter million dollars, had been donated by the North American Foundation for Wild Sheep, based in the northwestern United States. So, in fact, foreign hunters were actually paying the government of British Columbia to kill wolves.

Moreover, the Environment Minister, himself a big game hunter, was the elected Legislative Member for the Peace River district where the wolf-kill took place. A personal friend of his, a local outfitter, who had donated one hundred thousand dollars to the minister's political party, had obtained the contract of housing the wolf-killers in his fly-in hunting lodge on Scoop Lake, deep in the wilderness. Local businessmen in private aircraft were assisting the government hunters by scouting for wolves and by radioing their location to the helicopter. It was even rumored that local hunters had shot moose for bait and placed them on frozen lakes to lure wolf packs into the open where they could be shot easiest.

When questioned, the B.C. Wildlife Branch had no choice but to admit the basics of its predator control campaign. Starting in January 1984, government biologists had begun a 5-year program of wolf reduction in the Kechika and Muskwa regions of the Peace country, northwest of Fort St. John. The target for the first winter was 300-400 wolves to be shot from the air by government biologists in helicopters.

Enter one of the world's most courageous and radical animal activists, Paul Watson, a curly-haired, chubby young man with strong opinions and a tough resolve. Paul had been one of the original crusaders with Greenpeace, now a respected global environmental organisation. Originally, the group had been launched in British Columbia to protest American nuclear testing in Alaskan waters. Soon it was heavily involved in the whaling issue. Paul Watson, expert seaman, had sailed on Greenpeace's flagship the Rainbow Warrior and he had played a leading role in the scuttling of whaling ships in their Icelandic harbour. His extremist and sometimes illegal tactics eventually led to his departure from Greenpeace and to the formation of his own group, the Sea Shepherd Society. When the wolf-kill controversy hit the media, Paul started Project Wolf and formed a coalition with other environmental groups, mostly American, to fight the B.C. government, in the streets, in the courts, and in the field.

While his allies were waving placards on the steps of legislatures and in front of Canadian embassies abroad, urging a tourist boycott of British Columbia, Paul set out to meet the wolf-killers head-on, in the wilds of the Peace district. Apart from personal courage and conviction, and despite a lack of experience in the bush, his most effective weapon was the international news media which shadowed him all the way.

In the dead of winter, on February 4, 1984, Paul led a small band of followers to Fort Nelson, a hamlet of hunters, trappers and Indians at milepost 300 along the Alaska Highway. The "wolf defenders" got a rough reception. Townsfolk were openly hostile, refusing to sell accommodation and gasoline. Paul's idea was to charter an aircraft, to locate the headquarters of the wolf-killers on remote Scoop Lake, and to confront biologist John Elliott who was in charge of the operation. His companions intended to chain themselves to the helicopter, preventing it from taking off. And Paul would try to actively interfere with the hunt by flying near and in front of the helicopter. But no-one wanted to rent him a plane. The group organised a meeting with local people to explain their views. It was attended by an overflow crowd. After much shouting and heckling, the heated exchange ended in pandemonium when a local hunter threw a dead wolf onto the podium. It was all duly caught on the cameras of international television.

Paul's next plan was to reach Elliott's wolf-hunting lodge on foot, by hiking and snowshoeing nearly 100 km (62 miles) through roadless wilderness. The trek was started from the Alaska highway where it parallels the Liard River. News crews were standing on the snow-packed road, stamping their feet and smacking their gloved hands together, grumbling about the cold, when the band of seven protesters slid down the steep river bank. They were soon out of sight, carrying heavy packs, an axe, a small rifle and a tiny two-way radio. Their snowshoes were of little help in the deep snow and dense bush. By nightfall, they had covered no more than two or three kilometers. The temperature dropped to minus thirty degrees Celsius (-20 F.), while a million stars blazed in the clear sky. Silence, the total silence of wilderness, closed in.

Paul's band had trouble sleeping and keeping warm, lying in their bags under a tree by a drafty fire. One of the young men had stepped through overflow ice on the river and had got his feet wet. After he took his boots off in an attempt to dry them, they froze solid. Severely frost-bitten and at the point of a mental breakdown, he had to be helped out the following morning. Two more members dropped out the next day, unable to cope with the frigid conditions.

The trek was aborted on the third day when news reached the group that a helicopter had been made available. However, it developed mechanical trouble before Paul and his men could reach their goal. A few days later Watson decided to cancel further attempts and to return to Vancouver. Despite all setbacks and disappointments, he claimed partial victory. "We exposed the fact that the wolf-hunt was being conducted only to benefit the outfitters. We also managed to keep the issue before the international press, and we learned how to deal with the hunt the next time, when we will have our own aircraft lined up." Paul and his group Project Wolf would continue to support a tourist boycott against the province and seek a legal injunction against the hunt.

In the meantime, how did the British Columbia government defend itself against the onslaught of media attention and public indignation? It handed out press releases and scientific reports, and replaced its Minister of the Environment. His successor assured the public that the wolf control program had been misunderstood and distorted by those who appeared to be ignorant of the wolf's true nature. But opposition to the B.C. wolf-kill was not only coming from the general public. In March of 1984, two professional organizations of biologists, the Wildlife Society of Canada and the Canadian Society of Zoologists, released an independent assessment of the predator control program, based on the examination of detailed research information obtained from the B.C. Ministry of Environment. The societies believed that there was no justification for wolf control and that "the science of wildlife biology has been misrepresented in the minister's news releases and compromised the role of wildlife biologists." In addition to the broadsides from their peers, the B.C. wildlife managers received letters from some 9,000 irate citizens and nearly 200 environmental groups from across North America and even Europe. Never before had the B.C.

government received so much mail on any one subject.

Quite suddenly, in September of 1985, the new Minister of the Environment, Austin Pelton, announced that wolves would no longer be shot from the air in B.C. "If the need arises, we will remove predators probably by localized trapping, but not by aerial methods."

However, rumors about an impending resumption of the helicopter flights persisted during the fall of that year. The *Sun* revealed that it had obtained a Wildlife Branch report dated July 1986 and authored by biologist John Elliott, who stated that "the suspension of wolf removal in the Muskwa area has quickly resulted in a shift in the wolf/prey balance." The wolf population had increased three-fold. In an interview with the *Sun* he said that "to ensure the success of the wolf-kills of 1982-1985, which were followed by increased survival of moose and elk calves, the wolf-kill must be continued." He believed that the potential for trapping was limited because of the terrain, and shooting from helicopters was more humane anyway. "Would you rather sit in a trap?" he asked. And he added that he was waiting for a decision from Environment Minister Pelton to resume aerial wolf-kills in the Muskwa.

Elliott boarded his helicopter gunship on the first of February. He intended to "remove" 200 wolves from the Muskwa, a remote region of some 14,000 km² (5,500 miles²), of mountains, wide valleys and deep forests, where the biologist had estimated the wolf population at 350-500. How many wolves he actually killed during the next two months was kept secret, because regional wildlife managers were no longer allowed to handle news media enquiries and the head office in Victoria was not giving out any more "body counts." According to a ministry spokesman, "reporting body counts sounded like the Vietnam war. It's one of the things people react to in an emotional way. It is in the Branch's interest to give out details after a wildlife program." In other words, the ministry wanted to do its job without further interference from the press or the public.

Meanwhile, Paul Watson acknowledged that his new group Friends of the Wolf was powerless to impede the recently begun Muskwa wolf-kill, but he was not giving up. His group planned to be less confrontational than its predecessor Project Wolf in the hope that the new approach would win wider public support. His earlier calls for international tourist boycotts had led to some criticism from friends and foes alike. It was said that Paul's tough stand had been counter-productive and had raised the hackles of many people who would otherwise support the cause.

Nevertheless, the demonstrations continued. On Valentine's day, some 40 placard-carrying friends of the wolf demonstrated at Fantasy Gardens, a theme park run by B.C. Premier Bill VanderZalm. A dozen people staged a brief protest in London, England, during the premier's trip to Europe. VanderZalm was unimpressed. He explained the problem in his characteristic folksy way: "We have people moving in with guns, hunters... who are hunting for certain species...and the wolves get left because nobody wants one over the mantelpiece. I am not a hunter, but I can appreciate that one day, if you go out to kill the moose and the deer and the elk, and leave the wolves, one day you are going to have an imbalance...We don't have nature taking care of things."

It was becoming increasingly clear that the controversy surrounding the B.C. wolf-kills was polarizing between hunters and non-hunters. However, despite all publicity, the combatants appeared to have reached a stalemate. Elliott continued to shoot wolves from the air, and the wolf defenders went on protesting, hoping for reinforcement from the western United States, where wolves and wolf reintroduction were gaining in popularity. During the winter of 1987-88, Friends of the Wolf affiliates were organized from Washington State down to California. Seven members of the California group, some of them in elaborate wolf costumes, chained themselves to desks in the Canadian Consulate building in Los Angeles. The day before, a member of the local Wolf Liberation Army had thrown a "blood" bomb onto the ice of the hockey area where the Vancouver Canucks played the Los Angeles Kings.

A mixed group of American and Canadian wolf defenders set up a tent in the offices of the B.C. government in Victoria and chained themselves to the desk of the new Environment Minister, Bruce Strachan, the fourth to be appointed to the beleaguered portfolio in three years. More adventurous protesters from the United States were heading out into the field to try to interfere with the wolf-kill. A group of activists from Montana drove north via cities in B.C. and Alberta and held demonstrations at shopping centers and universities along the way. Three female university students from Los Angeles flew to Vancouver where they consulted with Paul Watson and chartered a plane for Fort Nelson. The idea was to locate Elliott's camp. The young women had received training as parachutists and planned to stage a drop-in for the benefit of a television crew. But neither the parachutists nor the protest caravan from Montana managed to locate the wolf-killer's new headquarters. The stunts and demonstrations toughened the minister's resolve. "Having Americans telling British Columbians about environmental policy is totally hypocritical." The protestors were equally determined and they had another arrow on their bow. On March 6, 1988, Friends of the Wolf in partnership with a new powerful ally, the Western Canada Wilderness Committee, achieved a major breakthrough. They took the Environment Department to court and asked this simple question: Since hunting and shooting from the air is illegal in the province, how did a government biologist obtain a permit to kill wolves from a helicopter?

Supreme Court justice Carol Huddart reviewed the case and ruled the permit invalid, much to the surprise of everyone involved. Thus, after four years of arguments and demonstrations, after an avalanche of letters, reports and press releases, the wolf-kill was stopped cold by a technicality of law. Silence descended again over the wolf defender's western front.

Part III

PREDATORS, PREY AND PEOPLE

Freed from the shackles of our past,
we can return to wolves and wilderness
on our own terms,
for our renewal and their preservation.

Chapter 13

THE MANAGEMENT DILEMMA

Speaking on behalf of the provincial Trappers Association, the portly man behind the microphone ridiculed environmentalists who, according to him, wanted to protect wolves until all hoofed animals were gone. "Pretty soon, all we have left are wolves!" Throwing up his hands in an exaggerated gesture of sincerity, he added: "What are they going to eat?"

"Trappers!" shouted a voice from the audience. It was one of very few moments of droll hyperbole in the serious proceedings of the Vancouver Wolf Symposium, held at the University of British Columbia on May 10-11, 1988. Jointly sponsored by the Faculty of Forestry, the B.C. Wildlife Branch and the Northwest Wildlife Preservation Society, the symposium had been organized in response to the public outcry over the aerial wolf-kills conducted by provincial biologists during the previous five years. The event drew several hundred delegates from a wide spectrum of interest groups: government wildlife agencies, university biologists, hunters, trappers, tourism associations, native people, and environmentalists of all stripes.

As expected, points of view varied greatly and were sharply

polarized in two camps, either for or against wolf control. While environmentalists waxed eloquent about wolves and wilderness, groups with an axe to grind, particularly hunters, trappers and outfitters, minimized the killing of wolves as a necessary evil. There were much greater dangers threatening our rich wildlife heritage, they said, such as large-scale mining and forestry developments. "Let us not fiddle while Rome burns!" was the new rallying cry coined by Alaska moose biologist Bill Gasaway. He posed that natural densities of large mammals in the northwoods were quite low and that they had been brought even lower by the combination of hunting and predation. Wolf control was "an effective management tool" to boost the inventories of big game to much higher levels, in Alaska as well as Canada, creating a source of revenue from hunting that would make legislators think twice before opening the door to resource extraction companies and despoil the wilderness.

The notion was adapted eagerly by those who were already in favor of wolf control. Jim Walker, director of the B.C. Wildlife Branch, emphasized that economic arguments determine the outcome of resource decisions in the province. "If you are really concerned about wolves, don't parachute into the Muskwa to face John Elliott. Parachute into those land-use meetings with the developers!"

Government biologist Dale Seip, one of the principal organizers of the symposium, gave an overview of the dynamics of wolf-prey systems. If ungulate populations, for whatever reason, were at very low densities, much below the carrying capacity of their habitat, wolves could prevent recovery and keep their prey in a so-called low equilibrium, popularly called a "predator pit." The objective of management was to get the system out of this low equilibrium and into a high equilibrium. And the quickest way to do that was through wolf control. As soon as positive results had been achieved, i.e. a large increase in hoofed mammals, controls could be relaxed. This theory remains the basic justification for government programs to kill wolves across Canada and Alaska. Wildlife managers admit that recovery of prey numbers could also take place through natural means, such as a spontaneous decline of wolf numbers, but such a cyclic adjustment would take years, presumably well over a decade. Artificial control of wolves would bring the desired results much quicker. And in the final analysis, everybody was supposed to be well-served, hunters as well as wolf lovers, since the high densities of hoofed mammals would allow a return of the predators to greater numbers than before. However, Bill Gasaway warned that prey and predators would not remain abundant in the absence of some kind of long-term management; wolf populations could recover rapidly from temporary control.

This latter point, the resilience of wolf populations, was one of the key counter arguments of those opposing control. Large-scale killing would shatter wolf societies and allow more pairs to breed, free from the restraints imposed by the hierarchy of territorial packs. Given a rich prey base, the wolf population would rebound quickly, perhaps to greater levels than before. This was exactly the scenario described by John Elliott, the B.C. government biologist who had been at the eye of the storm of public indignation which had forced the B.C. Wildlife Branch to quit the aerial killing. In his presentation, Elliott said that despite his control efforts, there had been a steady increase of wolves in the "treatment" areas, partly by a high rate of reproduction and partly by immigration from surrounding "untreated" areas. "Or it may relate to a reduction in illegal killing once we got the program going." Apparently, some northern residents - hunters or trappers - had been doing their own wolf control in the bush, unknown to anyone but their closest allies. These people were thought to have stopped their clandestine activities when they learned that the government was monitoring wolf densities in the backwoods in preparation for control.

Speaking in a low monotone, Elliott assessed the success of his aborted wolf-kill program as follows: "It's obvious, pulse management, periodic killing of wolves, as we did in the Kechika is a waste of time. All it does is increase the predator/prey fluctuations. So that's not going to work. However, if we do nothing, we are going to be looking at a pretty simple future out there: small numbers of ungulates, moderate numbers of wolves." Thus, rather ironically, Elliott himself believed that the controversial action in which he personally had shotgunned 996 wolves from helicopters, had been a failure because he had been forced to quit after five years.

Among the symposium speakers were several other biologists reporting on ongoing wolf control actions. In a data-studded presentation from the Yukon, biologist Bob Hayes gave some preliminary results of a game management program in the Finlayson mountains where a declining herd of woodland caribou had recovered from 2,500 to 7,500 after seven years of aerial wolf control. In contrast to the international outcry raised against the aerial killings in British Columbia, the Yukon program had largely escaped public criticism. During the implementation of the controls, the government biologists had obtained the cooperation of local Indians, who had voluntarily reduced their hunting kill of caribou from several hundred per year to just a few dozen. The simultaneous reduction in the levels of hunting and predation had indeed produced the desired increase in the herds.

It may come as a surprise that native people are not necessarily against wolf control of any kind. At the Vancouver symposium, the Indian representative declared his support for aerial shooting with this statement: "Everything must be managed, wolves included!" Alaska natives admitted that they had practised their own form of wolf control for years by the so-called denning method, the killing of pups at known wolf dens. In the Northwest Territories, on the wide open tunda, aboriginal people on snowmobiles hunt down wolves by following their tracks.

During the 1990s, the alleged success of the Finlayson project in Yukon gave rise to Indian requests for a similar program in the Aishihik mountains where caribou estimates had plummeted to

500 with a very low calf survival rate of less than 10 per 100 cows. Aerial wolf control, in combination with voluntary restrictions on native hunting of caribou, began in the winter of 1992/1993. This time, the kill immediately ran into flak from animal rights groups, but the Yukon held firm. At least for awhile, until the international wolf defenders, freed from a successful fight in Alaska, began to focus their unrelenting attention on the Canadian Territory.

The day of aerial wolf killing appears to be over in Yukon, as it is elsewhere, unless the Indians begin a propaganda war of their own. There is no doubt that some Yukon tribes want wolf control. In February of 1993, when activist Paul Watson and half a dozen other Friends of the Wolf met with the Aishihik Indian band to question the wolf kill, the protesters received a welcome that was far from friendly. Retreating quickly, the leader of the group reported: "We were met with overt hostility and racism... and we were called meddling Europeans."

Based on conditions spelled out in ancient treaties, Canadian Indians have the right to hunt game for subsistence anywhere on public lands without bag limits or seasonal restrictions. There is little doubt that First Nations, as aboriginal people like to call themselves, will play an increasingly important role in the future management of wolves and their prey species, all across the North and West, hopefully for the better of all.

Chapter 14

RAIDERS IN THE NIGHT

"I hate wolves!" muttered the young country woman as she examined her favorite colt. Its flanks were streaked with blood, oozing out of a deep wound in the rump. A chunk of skin and flesh, almost the size of a football, had been cleanly bitten out of the colt's buttock, as if it had been cut with a knife. During the night, no-one had paid attention to the brief barking of the dog. And the running of horses had been lost in the roar of the November wind rattling in the poplars by the house. Turning off the light before going to bed, as was his nightly ritual, the rancher had glanced outside just as a cloud passed before the moon and the sleek predators that ran by the corral vanished into shadow. The dog did not return during the day. Much later, its collar was found some distance away on the brushy pasture.

For people who live in the northwoods, on the edge of wilderness, attitudes toward wolves depend on whose ox is being gored. The staunchest friend of all things natural may change his or her mind after experiencing first-hand what predators can do to livestock and pets. Wolves have been a threat to the interests of homesteaders ever since North America was settled, and they continue to be a regional concern in the northern portions of all Canadian provinces, from Quebec to British Columbia, as well as in Minnesota and the northwest.

Opposition from the ranching industry was the major stumbling block frustrating the long-postponed reintroduction of wolves to Yellowstone, despite assurances that livestock owners would be compensated for any losses suffered. Apparently, it is much more difficult to build tolerance for the predators in areas where the species went extinct long ago than it is in regions where local people still know and accept it as part of nature. In fact, on the fringes of northern agriculture, the incidence of wolf predation on livestock is not all that high. And the great majority of wolves in Canada and the northeastern states, even those that live in livestock regions, prefer venison and rarely dine on beef.

Detailed figures published by British Columbia reveal that there are about 1,500 cattle and sheep operations located within provincial wolf range and that less than 2.5 percent experience predation problems. In Alberta, where about 300,000 cattle summer on wolf range, less than 0.03 percent, mostly calves, are reported lost per year. The interface of agriculture and forest is particularly extensive in Minnesota where there are about 7,000 farms within wolf range, but only 0.33 percent report trouble with the predators that kill less than 0.02 percent of available cattle and sheep per year. Thus, livestock operations on the wilderness fringe are clearly not endangered by wolves.

However, some individual operations can be hit hard and repeatedly, particularly if wolves learn to prey on livestock. In some regions, government agencies can be to blame by opening up remote and marginal lands for homesteading or summer grazing leases. In other cases, the blame lies with the farmers themselves if they allow their cows to calve on lands where supervision is difficult. It is also a bad idea to leave the carcasses of dead cattle out in the field, giving predators a taste of beef. Sound husbandry methods and responsible care for livestock are prerequisites for avoiding predation problems in the first place.

How do citizens and governments deal with legitimate cases of livestock losses if they occur despite all precaution? A few provinces and states, such as Ontario and Minnesota, have instituted a damage indemnity fund run by civil servants who evaluate the complaint and assist ranchers or farmers in applying for financial compensation at fair market rates. Most jurisdictions employ predator control officers who specialize in removing the offending wolves. The preferred method in eastern provinces and states is trapping or snaring. The captured animal is then either killed or released in far-off wildlands.

In Minnesota, between 1975 and 1986, the number of wolves killed in livestock damage operations used to be about 22 per year, just over one percent of the state's population. However after 1993, an increase in predators was coupled with an increase in problems and well over one hundred wolves were trapped yearly and killed by lethal injection. In British Columbia, wildlife officers still use poison. From 1978 to 1981, an average of 113 wolves were destroyed per year. During 1988-1990, government agents placed a total of 799 baits and an estimated 439 were taken by wolves. How many died was not exactly known since the kind of poison used (1080) allowed the scavengers to get away before succumbing, making them difficult to find.

In neighboring Alberta between 1972 and 1990, the average yearly kill of wolves in livestock damage cases was 67, mostly by poisoning. For Saskatchewan and Manitoba, where the interface of wilderness and agricultural lands is more abrupt than in Alberta, the number of wolves poisoned and trapped in livestock conflicts is reported to be 20-40 annually.

Why can Ontario, Quebec, Minnesota, Alaska and Montana manage their problem wolves without resorting to poison? And why do the western provinces continue to use these vile substances that often result in the death of so-called non-target species? The answer is that poison is cheap and effective, and that local people do not oppose it. In 1978-1980, British Columbia's Wildlife Branch observed a moratorium on the use of poison and chose other means such as trapping and shooting by helicopter, which proved to be less effective in stopping livestock damage complaints. Dissatisfied ranchers reacted by not bothering to report their losses and by taking the law into their own hands, setting illegal baits themselves until the government resumed their use.

In the mountainous interior of British Columbia, ranches occupy narrow valleys hemmed in by forested hills where large carnivores are common. Should the government react to every wolf report with preventive action? Sometimes they do. In one isolated case, along a 20 km (12 miles) section of river valley where local ranchers had suffered very little real damage, 71 wolves were killed over a four-year period. The validity of such preventive control is questionable. The constant removal of wolves not responsible for livestock damage is unlikely to resolve

the perceived problem. On the contrary; as other wolves move in to replace the "good" wolves that were killed off, some of the newcomers may include a renegade that indeed turns to killing livestock. Instead of always giving in to demands for preventive control, wildlife agents in B.C. and elsewhere have learned to act only in a reactive fashion, after it has been established that there is indeed a proven case of predation.

To prevent trouble, individual ranchers can take several measures themselves, all of them non-lethal, such as frequent supervision of herds and their enclosure in fenced corrals during winter or at calving time. Some people have experimented with the installation of deterrent devices, such as bright ribbons, flashing lights or sirens, that are supposed to scare off intruders, but little is known about their true merit. One of the latest methods involves the use of ultrasonic whistles. Unfortunately, after some initial success, predators become used to the sound. To minimize the chance of habituation, researchers in Nova Scotia have developed the "wailer" that emits a variable range of ultrasonic frequencies. Testing in Nova Scotia reduced coyote predation on sheep. However, it remains to be seen whether a modified version of this gadget would have any effect on wolves.

Taste aversion techniques involve the placing of baits of mutton or beef containing an additive that causes the scavenger to become ill, conditioning it to avoid further use of such foods. Again, the effectiveness of this method is largely unproven in the case of wolves.

Another, much heralded system of deterring predation on sheep and goats involves the use of livestock guarding dogs, an ancient method that dates back thousands of years and is still practiced in Italy and Spain, where suitable breeds have been developed. Although they may weigh more than 50 kg (110 lbs), as much as the heaviest wolf, these dogs have a very weak predatory nature. They would not even chase a ball! They owe their effectiveness to just being there with the grazing animals. Coyotes simply avoid trouble and stay away. But again, the system has yet to be tested with wolves, especially those in northern habitats which are much bigger than the smallish wolves of southern Europe.

As an experiment, Raymond Coppinger, one of the principal advocates of livestock guarding dogs, established a bait station in the Minnesota forest. Soon, wolves came to feed every night. After a month, a dog was confined to the area by a so-called invisible fence that sent a radio-signal to the dog's collar, delivering an electric tingle if it came too close. The dog was to guard the bait. The wolves continued to come and looked at him from a distance every night, gradually approaching closer. On the 28th day, there was a fight and the dog was chased down the road until it found shelter in a building. However, when the same dog was given a companion, the two held off the pack indefinitely. Like wolves, the dog is a social animal that finds comfort and strength in company.

The effectiveness of livestock guarding dogs depends on their handlers and on their training. As puppies they have to be raised with the kind of stock they are to guard, to make them feel like one of the herd, either sheep, goats or cattle. There are already several thousand of these dogs taking care of livestock in the U.S. where their major adversary is the coyote. It remains to be seen whether a pack of large western wolves can be repelled by their domestic brothers. If so, it would offer hope for the eventual resolution of an age-old conflict that is bound to flare up again locally, now that the notorious raiders are returning to more of their former range.

Chapter 15

A QUESTION OF GHOSTS

The "Gray Ghost of the Northwoods", as Canadian field biologists have dubbed it, has been venerated for a very long time. Already 15,000 years ago, palaeolithic tribes of the Cro-magnon era painted its portrait on the walls of caves in Spain and France, the first known examples of wildlife art. Historians usually call it just a deer, but the shape of the curved antlers that send a palmated tine forward over the animal's cow-like face, leave no doubt as to its true identity: caribou, or reindeer as the species is known in the Old World. At the time when the cave murals were painted, the caribou lived as far north as the ice age permitted, at the edge of the great glaciers that covered much of northern Europe. Today, after the ice has retreated, its boreal range stretches across the frigid top of the world, from Norway to Siberia and from Alaska to Labrador.

An extremely successful member of the cervids or deer family, the caribou is well-adapted to life in the North, with a dense coat of hollow hairs that insolate it from the bitter cold, and with large round hooves that carry it over snow and marshy ground. To better take advantage of local conditions, it has developed into several sub-species that vary in size from the tiny Peary caribou of the high arctic islands to the sturdy woodland race of boreal forests and muskeg. The most numerous is the medium-sized barren-ground caribou. In this century, its once great herds dwindled through overhunting to alarming lows in the 1950s, when it looked like the species was on the way out, until they began an almost miraculous recovery. Today, the total North American population is estimated at close to three million, and immense herds again cover the tundra during their twice-yearly migrations to and from arctic calving grounds.

In southern Canada, concern for the species now centers on the most solitary and the biggest of the clan, the woodland caribou. A western bull can reach up to 270 kg (600 lbs), more than twice as much as his arctic cousins. After European settlement of North America, the distribution of the heavy-weight recluse of the woods has shrunk far back in latitude and it now occurs only sporadically in some pockets of good habitat south of the 55th parallel. Recently, the elusive "gray ghost" has played a critical role in the ongoing debate about its ancient enemy, the wolf. Unless wolves were controlled, some scientists warned, the last of the woodland caribou in southern Ontario, Alberta and British Columbia would become extirpated.

A real shocker exploded onto the public consciousness in the fall of 1986 when the Alberta government published its *Caribou Restoration Plan* detailing the species' decline in the province's western foothills. Since 1966, the population in Willmore Wilderness, north of Jasper National Park, had dwindled from an estimated 1,200-1,800 to less than 300! Unless measures were taken immediately to protect remnant herds, the report's author claimed, the woodland caribou was doomed to extinction. Annual losses from all causes were estimated at 22 percent and the reproductive rate at only 15 percent.

"There is a clear deficit, the population is in decline and we are running out of time," insisted biologist Janet Edmonds. She admitted that she had not studied the area's wolf population but she knew enough to say that the predators were common and that they were taking too many caribou. Therefore, she proposed to kill up to 70 percent of the wolves on the caribou's range for three to four years. And the best way to achieve that was through the use of helicopter shooting.

The proposal was leaked to the press and raised a storm of protest from the public and environmental groups. The Sierra Club of Canada called a meeting in Calgary, attended by over 1,200 people, who were addressed by Farley Mowat. When he took the stage, the famous author placed his hands at his mouth and gave an ear-splitting wolf howl. In his presentation he lambasted government biologists and hunters alike who were all "in the business of killing wildlife, just for the hell of it." His mixture of droll humor and hard-hitting opinion was followed by a showing of the hilarious film *Never Cry Wolf*, based on his best-selling book. The meeting received a lot of media exposure and the government backed down quickly from the wolf-kill idea.

However, during the next few years, the issue popped back up in the news again and again as government biologists reiterated their alarming theory that the woodland caribou, which had recently been added to the growing list of threatened species, would become locally extinct unless action was began at once. And one of the most urgent steps to be taken was a return to wolf control.

Unfortunately, the biologists failed to place the Alberta caribou question in its proper perspective. They did not explain to the public that moose, elk and deer had also declined steeply during the same period. And that the cause was a combination of factors, not only predation, but mainly severe winters, hunting and the opening up of former wilderness by resource developments. In recent decades, the forests and mountains of western Alberta had been torn open by an exploding network of lumber roads and seismic lines, exposing hoofed animals to increasing pressure from hunters and poachers, who had become far more mobile than before on newly acquired all-terrain vehicles, snowmobiles, trikes and buggies. In the formerly closed forests north of Jasper, where the "gray ghost" used to lead a secluded life, it was now even at risk of colliding with trucks and cars on the new highway that had been constructed to the booming coal-mining town of Grande Cache, right across the caribou's migration route.

While some of the above factors were acknowledged in the Restoration Plan, its author stated bluntly that "wolf predation was the primary cause of the continued decline." Moreover, she said, the caribou had become even more vulnerable today than formerly, since the cutting of mature forests in much of its winter range had led to improved habitat for moose and deer, which in turn could support more wolves. While healthy moose were capable of defending themselves against attack, biologists believed that caribou were weak and the wolves would pick them off one by one, until none remained.

This scary but deceptively logical scenario sounded believable to many people and began to erode opposition to the wolf control proposals, even among naturalists. What harm would it do to kill a few wolves, they said, if it meant saving the caribou? The notion soon converted major environmental groups, such as World Wildlife Fund and the Canadian Nature Federation, which announced that they would not oppose local wolf control if it was done in the interest of protecting a threatened species. But they had a few conditions: the controls would have to be temporary and all hunting on caribou had to be suspended simultaneously. In fact, to its credit, the Alberta government had already stopped the season on woodland caribou in 1981. Unfortunately, hunters often shot it by mistake, taking it for a moose or elk. And native people and poachers continued to kill caribou along roads and highways where the animals often lingered, partly because of good grazing and partly because it allowed a refuge from natural predators.

Equally alarming statements about the imminent demise of woodland caribou came from interior British Columbia. The message was that moose were spreading higher into mountains where they had been scarce before, attracting wolves that preyed in proportion more heavily on the few remaining caribou. This theory had first been advanced by veteran caribou biologist Tom Bergerud. To test his hypothesis, B.C. government biologist Dale Seip conducted a detailed six-year study in which he compared caribou mortality in two areas that had a different species composition. In the Quesnel Highlands, moose, caribou and wolves shared the same summer range. In the other study area, Wells Gray Provincial Park, the caribou migrated in spring to high alpine terrain while most of the moose and wolves stayed behind in the lower valleys.

During each of the six years of his research, Seip and his helpers netted and radio-collared between 16 and 26 adult female caribou, as well as several moose and wolves. The transmitters were fitted with a sensor that gave a different signal if the animal stopped moving. The objective was to find out how many of the caribou died, and why. The results were monitored from the air by regular helicopter surveys.

In the Quesnel Highlands, where caribou, moose and wolves shared the range during summer, the caribou had a yearly mortality rate of 29 percent and very few calves survived to October, less than three per hundred cows. By contrast, in Wells Gray Park, where caribou moved away from moose and wolves during summer, adult mortality was only 8 percent and up to 37 percent of cows were still accompanied by their calves in October. Spring calf production in these two caribou populations was roughly the same; about half of the adult females had calves in June, but in the Quesnel Highlands most of the calves were gone by autumn. The exact cause of death was often difficult or impossible to tell. Bear predation was a significant factor in both study areas but the heaviest losses were associated with wolf presence.

To test whether or not wolf control would make a difference, Seip reduced the Quesnel wolf population by shooting and trapping, which indeed led to improved calf survival. Before wolf control, only one of 40 radio-collared caribou cows had a calf by October; after control, 9 of 23 had surviving calves by autumn. Seip concluded his report with the following warning: "If present trends continue, the remaining caribou populations that spend the summer in highland areas will be eliminated, and only those caribou that migrate to rugged, mountainous habitat for the summer will survive." It sums up the case for the woodland caribou; it can only survive in the right habitat, especially during the critical period when its young are born.

More compelling evidence for the caribou-versus-moose theory emerged from Ontario. In a technical note published by the Ministry of Natural Resources, L. Godwin wrote that predation, mainly by wolves, was the most significant mortality factor affecting the 15,000 or so woodland caribou that still occur across the province's north where moose are scarce. In this rather simple ecosystem, caribou were the only winter prey of wolves and wolf numbers were limited by the number of caribou, and vice-versa. However, of special concern were six remnant caribou herds, totalling about 500 animals, along Lake Superior and in Pukaskwa National Park. In this more complicated southern ecosystem, moose are an alternate winter prey and wolf density is therefore not dependent upon caribou. And where moose are common, the report stated, wolves can become numerous enough "to hunt caribou to the last animal."

Is the woodland recluse really as vulnerable as biologists tell us? Does it have no specialized strategy, as other prey species have, to cope with or minimize predation? If it did not, would it have managed to coexist with its ancient enemy for so long? Let us review what is known about caribou behavior.

Like all creatures that live in a natural environment, the caribou's primary concern is to stay away from predators and to shield its young. It does so in a unique way by isolating itself in barren environments where few other members of the deer family and their predators can live. In contrast to what is commonly believed, caribou are not specialized feeders that can only thrive on a diet of lichens, but they also eat a wide variety of herbaceous plants, grasses and sedges, leaves and twigs of trees and shrubs, as well as mushrooms. In fact, the caribou is a more versatile forager than any other ungulate and it manages to survive where no other hoofed mammal can, even on the barren grounds and in old-growth timber where the only ground cover is a gray lichen, called caribou moss. In snow, the caribou with its large hooves has the amazing ability to dig deep craters, right down to the ground. If the snow is hard and crusted, the animal can even subsist on arboreal lichens that hang like a scruffy black beard from spruce and pine. So, in a way, the caribou has many arrows on its bow. By virtue of its catholic feeding habits it can distance itself from moose, deer and elk, as well as from their associated predators.

By the same token, woodland caribou should never become too numerous themselves. If the herds grow too large, they might constitute a substantial prey base for wolves that will learn to follow them to their hidden hang-outs and to their calving grounds, hunting the new-born with selective determination. Woodland caribou have to be few and far between, lost in space so to speak, so that it will not pay for the wolf to search for them. The law of diminishing returns would force the predator to go where the chance of finding food is greater than the loss of energy associated with the search.

For that reason, in my opinion, it would have been a grave mistake to begin wolf control in western Alberta after caribou numbers had dropped to the low levels of today. The large numbers of the 1960s were "unnaturally" high, an artifact of fifteen years of wolf poisoning. Then, after predator controls stopped, the wolves came back with a vengeance and followed the caribou to their calving grounds in the high mountains of Willmore and Jasper. The herds had only one way to go: down. Eventually, their numbers readjusted to the low level that the area can really support, and wolf presence became far less on the calving grounds. A return to predator control, as some biologists had advocated for so long, would have started another unnatural cycle that was best avoided in the first place. The above theories of mine, first presented in 1986, have since been advanced by several biologists. Even more heartening is the fact that Janet Edmonds reported in 1994 that the woodland caribou in the Willmore region were doing reasonably well and that her 1982 report had been too pessimistic.

If caribou have to be scarce in order to avoid attracting too much attention from predators, how to explain the great herds on the barren grounds? Given the enormous size of its habitat, the tundra caribou can afford to be abundant as long as it keeps moving. For the individual, there is safety in numbers. To protect the new-born, the herds make each spring long-distance migrations to calving areas on the arctic coasts, while most wolves stay behind near the tree-line to den and take care of their own young.

The need to avoid wolves during calving time is indeed of primary concern to all caribou. Those of lower latitudes make shorter journeys to localized refuges that offer protective isolation. In mountainous regions, caribou migrate in spring to the highest alpine grasslands, some of which may be a hundred miles distant from the wintering range. Those that live all year in woodlands have to make do with pockets of habitat that will serve the same function, discouraging moose, deer and wolves. Such conditions can be found only on islands, in large muskegs or in lichen-covered old-growth forests that have very little forage to support grazers and browsers.

How much or how little a caribou travels is of vital importance too. On the vast tundra, the barren-ground herds are always on the go, trotting with clicking hooves over rocky ground, wading through swamps and swimming the widest of rivers without hesitation. Feeding on the go, they never stay anywhere long enough to allow predators to build up in numbers. By contrast, the woodland caribou, which can only find a few pockets of good habitat in its year-round range, has to be sedentary, remaining in a few acres of suitable terrain as long as possible. The less it travels, the less chance that its tracks are found and followed by predators, and the less energy is wasted.

Especially during winter, the woodland caribou becomes like a ghost, barely moving, staying under cover of large spruce trees, its gray coat resembling the subdued colors of its chosen environment. Woodland caribou are best left alone. Over the millennia, their ancient ways have proven themselves. And all we humans can do, if we are serious about protection, is to save them large tracts of wilderness where they can be themselves, gray ghosts, hidden in the shrouded forest.

Chapter 16

TO KILL AND LET LIVE

The flames of a campfire dance and flicker in the darkness, an ever-changing play of light and shadow, mesmerizing the party of hunters huddled together, smoking, drinking and talking. While the chill of the autumn night deepens, they draw closer around the glowing coals and the conversation becomes more animated. What is the subject that makes their voices rise and become strident? Politics? Religion? No, wolves! The men argue and gesticulate until one of them sums up what most feel in their hearts about the age-old debate: "Every deer killed by a wolf is one less for the hunter!" It is a deep-rooted conviction of those who want all deer for themselves. But, as Sammy Davis Junior suggested in a popular song about other dogmatic beliefs: "It ain't necessarily so!"

In the absence of wolves, the deer might have died of other causes, such as malnutrition, disease or accident. After some reflection, most hunters will readily admit that there are circumstances when predators can even have a beneficial effect on a prey species. Yet, the hard-nosed attitude that derives from the old gospel of frontiersmen and range riders always resurfaces as the final argument. Admittedly, it is no doubt true, and you can only deny it at your peril, that a forest without wolves can be made to produce more deer than a forest with wolves. The conflict between hunters and predators, in Canada and the United States, especially in regions where the wild dogs are reoccupying former range, indeed boils down to a question of competition.

It is the wildlife manager's task to work out a balance, allotting a fair share of the venison pie to hunters while leaving enough for natural predators. There is certainly a great need for such an arrangement, a compromise that is workable and acceptable to the people concerned. As has been demonstrated all too often, the combination of hunting and poaching superimposed on natural predation can lead to very low populations of ungulates and to endless arguments between the various interest groups as to where the blame lies. Greed and ignorance are still the greatest threats to the wise use of renewable natural resources, in the woods, on the tundra, in wetlands, lakes and oceans.

How does the hunter's share of the deer herds compare to the toll taken by wolves today? The interrelationship of white-tails, predators and people was studied in great detail in Minnesota by biologist Todd Fuller. Over a period of five years, he radio-collared 143 deer. The vast majority of deaths, about 77 percent, were human-related! That included 54 percent by legal shooting, 14 percent by poaching, and 7 percent as a result of wounding and hunting loss. By comparison, only 10 percent of the deer were killed by wolves. The remaining 15 percent succumbed to dogs, other predators, vehicle collisions or unknown factors. During summer, fawn mortality from all causes was 62 percent, the majority probably predator-related, but not necessarily wolves, although their density was high at 4 per 100 km^2 (38 miles^2). However, black bear numbers were three or four times greater, and in addition, there were bobcats and some coyotes, which are all potential killers of deer.

In the face of such high losses, year-round, it is perhaps not surprising that the deer population in the Minnesota study area declined, from ten to about four per square kilometer, which Fuller blamed on the issuing of too many hunting permits, hence on poor wildlife management.

Granted, wildlife management is seldom easy because a major component of the equation is out of control at all times: the weather. In the northern portion of the white-tail's range, more than half of a population can starve in a few months if the snow is deep and crusted. During the winter of 1988-1989, forty thousand deer were in danger of succumbing in southern Manitoba, where there are no wolves, and where ten thousand deer can be expected to starve to death each winter. Shouldn't that be termed a failure of management? Wouldn't it have been better to thin out those deer before food shortage took its terrible toll?

On the whole, it seems that wolves are the least of the white-tail's problem. The species has managed to expand its range during the past century well to the north and west, despite predators. With proper management, the wily herbivore can be made to flourish despite predators, but the combination of overhunting and natural predation quickly spells disaster from two sides. This two-pronged hazard was explained by researchers from Quebec who have conducted the most ambitious field studies on wolves, deer and moose in Canada.

François Potvin and associates compared the diet and prey selection of wolves in two study areas, one with no hunting and many deer, the other with hunting and few deer. The Papineau-Labelle Reserve in the Laurentian hills, north of Ottawa, contained around 7,500 white-tails, about 3 per 1 km². In the Stubbs Lake area, deer occurred at less than 1 per 2 km². The researchers radio-collared 43 wolves, analyzed 1,166 scats and examined the remains of 296 deer over a period of five years. The big discovery had to do with selectivity of the kills.

Where the white-tails were numerous, the wolves selected

primarily fawns and older animals, but in times of scarcity, they killed mainly prime-age deer. In the latter case, wolf predation was said to have an anti-regulatory effect, a term first coined by Alaskan researchers. It meant that the number of wolves did not decline immediately after deer declined, but remained high for a number of years, depressing the deer even further. This lag in response was costly in terms of damage done. Moreover, wolf predation was no longer selective toward the young and old, as it was when prey were numerous. In the study area where deer were scarce, prime age animals were the last to be left and the wolves persisted in hunting them. This scenario existed in much of Quebec a few decades ago when deer numbers over large areas dropped to very low levels, before strict hunting quotas were imposed. Who was really to blame?

On the other hand, when deer populations were up, as shown by the situation in Papineau-Labelle Reserve, they were not limited by predation. The wolves failed to increase to a level where they might have caused a decline in prey. The factors holding wolf numbers back appeared to be self-imposed by social stress and competition, as evidenced by small territories, large packs and frequent dispersal of individuals. Evidently, predators and prey were not exactly in balance in either area, which was also demonstrated in other Quebec studies, as well as in Ontario and Minnesota.

Wolf-prey relationships become more complicated and difficult to study if there are more than one prey species. One of them may function as an alternate or buffer food source supporting wolves at high levels while they continue to select the other, less common, prey species. Potvin and his associates reported that the wolves in their two study areas fed mainly on moose calves and beaver during summer, but hunted exclusively deer during winter, even when they were scarce. At that time of year, beaver were not available and adult moose were thought to be too hard to kill for these smallish eastern wolves. Moose are indeed in quite a different category than deer...

Slowly dipping his antlers from side to side, demonstrating the great size of the palmated blades that alternately reflect the light of the moon, the bull moose steps into the forest opening. Snorting belligerently, he looms up in the dusk like an apparition out of the prehistoric past when mammoths and sabre-toothed tigers reigned over the land. Standing two meters (six feet) at the shoulder and weighing a thousand pounds, he is among the last of the giants, lord of the northwoods. Fearless and defiant, he dwarfs his canid enemies and never runs from them, a stubbornness that makes him vulnerable to humans who have always killed by treachery, from a distance, with arrows or bullets. Man, the unequal savage, will strike the bull down in the prime of his life, in the glory of his courting days for which he has prepared himself during the long summer of solitary existence.

Apart from the two-legged hunters, there are no natural predators that can take on a big moose in his prime. The cow, though lacking antlers, is no less formidable and perhaps even more of a fighter, agile and short-tempered. In defense of her calf, she can keep wolves at bay for hours. Many an adversary has been kicked and stomped to death. Yet, all across Canada and Alaska, moose meat is the main stay of wolves. How do they do it? They waste no time on vigorous individuals, but instead exploit the vulnerability of the young, the sinile or less than healthy. This process of selection makes moose and wolves particularly suitable as subjects for the study of a predator/prey relationship. There is, in fact, no lack of such studies.

In southwestern Quebec, where moose are the main year-round prey of wolves, biologists François Messier and Michel Crête radio-collared 54 members of 14 contiguous packs. During 2,000 hours of flying time over a period of five years, they made 4,600 location checks in three study areas that had different moose densities. The area with the least moose (17 per 100 km^2/38 miles^2) had intense hunting pressure and a low wolf density. These packs had poor reproductive success, a high incidence of death from malnutrition, frequent pack break-ups and extra-territorial excursions. The density of moose was apparently below the minimum threshold at which a wolf pack could do well and raise pups. In other words, the hunting pressure was so high that the wolves were almost starved out.

In the area where hunting was light, moose occurred at greater densities (37 per 100 km^2) and both the wolf and the moose populations were fairly stable. However, the researchers emphasized that this stabilization occurred at a level lower than the habitat could support. Even if hunting were to be totally suspended, moose would probably not increase beyond 40 per 100 km^2. They would be kept at that level by predation. But without predation, the researchers thought that moose densities could reach 200-400 per 100 km^2! However, the stability of such an artificially high population remained to be demonstrated. It could easily come crashing down as a result of some natural calamity such as winter starvation, ticks or disease.

Some of the Quebec findings were supported by the results of an Ontario study by Tom Bergerud and associates who surveyed moose and wolf populations in Pukaskwa National Park, a rugged boreal wilderness of almost 2,000 km^2 (760 miles^2) on the north shore of Lake Superior. Over five winters, the area contained 387-679 moose, which were the main prey of 14-29 wolves. Hunting was not allowed in the park, yet the moose did not increase beyond 20-36 per 100 km^2, quite similar to the densities reported from Quebec. The authors of the Ontario study presented a technical model that recognized that "predation leads to some kind of stability not inherent in the dynamics of the prey alone." This means that without predators the moose might have fluctuated from high to low, increasing periodically until natural causes led to a decline.

The most publicized, long-term and ongoing study of moose and wolves is located in Isle Royale National Park, a Michigan island of 540 km^2 (210 miles^2) in Lake Superior. Moose are the only resident ungulate and there is no hunting. The self-contained park seems the ideal outdoor laboratory to observe wolves and their prey without any interference from humans. Since 1959, the populations have been intensively monitored from the air and the ground. It is one of the few studies where none of the wolves was captured for collaring, at least not until 1988 when things suddenly began to go very wrong. Here is the story.

The first wolves arrived on the island during the severe winter of 1948 when at least one pair crossed the ice from the mainland of Canada. They began to multiply under the protective watch of the U.S. National Park Service. Leading wolf biologists, such as David Mech and Rolf Peterson, marvelled at the dynamics of the evolving predator-prey relationship. The main pack grew to 15-22 animals. Air-borne biologists often observed it on the hunt but it frequently failed to make a kill. Adult moose that faced their enemies and refused to run were let go. Only about one in ten moose that fled and were chased ended up as a victim of slashing fangs. The brunt of predation was taken by the vulnerable age classes, the young, the very old and the sick, that succumbed after a prolonged struggle, with wolves tearing at the flanks, rump, legs and even the pendulous nose.

The moose population, which had been growing to about 1,400 in the early 1970s, began to decline as the wolves increased, reaching a peak of 50 in 1980. Then, a sudden reversal set in. By 1982, there were only 14. But the scientists were not alarmed and predicted that numbers would rebound and stabilize once the moose population, currently young and healthy, would age and become vulnerable again to its predators. It was thought that the system would cycle every thirty years or so and that the upswing would begin in the late 1980s. By 1984, the wolves increased to 24, but instead of stabilizing, they declined again to 12 in 1988 and to a low of 7 in 1989. What was happening?

During the course of the study, a number of wolves had been found dead. Three had succumbed to malnutrition and eleven had been killed by other wolves. Aggression between the three or four packs on the island was evidently high, caused by increased competition for food. However, by the end of the decade, it became increasingly clear that food shortages were not at the core of the problem; the wolves failed to increase even after many moose began dying of malnutrition and infestations of winter ticks.

One theory suggested that a virus introduced to the island by domestic dogs had decimated the wolves. Four of them were trapped and examined; two contained anti-bodies to canine parvovirus, a fatal disease of young dogs; three had been exposed to canine hepatitis; and all four showed evidence of lyme disease. It indicated that the animals had been exposed to these viruses but their precise effect was unknown. However, after several years of study, the notion that disease was the major cause of the wolves' decline had to be discounted.

The other theory was that genetic loss was at the root of the population's failure to produce offspring. DNA analysis revealed that all wolves were descendants of a single female, perhaps one of the animals that crossed over to the island in 1948, leading to a high degree of relatedness among all wolves on the island, to low genetic variability and to a very low reproductive rate. Nevertheless, they managed to hang on with about a dozen adults and the occasional pup. By 1993, evidence of disease appeared to have diminished and food supply was expanding rapidly. Yet, some scientists thought that the famous wolves of Island Royale would eventually die out, unless new arrivals injected fresh blood and renewed vigor into the inbred clan. That possibility existed if a severe winter would again close the ice between the island and Canada, 24 km (15 miles) to the north. In any event, the park managers had decided not to intervene and to just watch the story unfold.

Quite unexpectedly, things suddenly began to improve. All three packs produced pups, bringing the total wolf number up to 22 by 1996! Again theories changed; genetic weakness had to be dismissed as the root cause of the earlier decline. The direct factor must have been parvovirus, and now that all evidence of the disease had disappeared, the wolves were free to increase again and take advantage of the ample food base. After reaching an all-time high of 2,400, the moose population had declined to less that 1,200 and there were numerous carcasses rotting in the woods.

All in all, it has become clear that the small size of the island and the wolves' isolation carry certain risks for scientific studies; prey-predator dynamics should be interpreted with the greatest of caution. On the mainland, long-distance dispersal is typical of wolves, particularly yearlings, which leads to the mixing of genes over vast expanses of land. This characteristic of wolf society was uncovered again and again during long-term and intensive telemetry research in Minnesota, Montana, Alberta and especially Alaska.

The "mother of all wolf studies", as Alaskan biologist Victor Van Ballenberghe termed it, was conducted by his colleagues in the Nelchina River basin, where over 250 wolves were radio-collared. It was also one of the most revealing studies of predation on moose. Wolf control, by aerial shooting in 1976-1978, had been followed by only small increases in calf survival, leading researchers to suspect that other factors were responsible for the low moose survival rates. Over 200 calves were radio-collared and their fates determined. The surprising discovery was that the major calf killers proved to be not wolves but bears, both grizzlies and blacks. These were particularly dangerous to moose calves because, as omnivores, bears are not limited by moose scarcity. Subsisting on vegetation, bears kill calves whenever the opportunity presents itself. They also search for them deliberately, even when they are scarce.

The despair of a mother moose facing a determined bear was observed first-hand by a couple of tourists in Jasper who had stopped to enjoy the mountain scenery at one of the viewpoints along the Icefield Parkway. Below them, in open terrain flanking a turbulent stream, they witnessed a drama unfold with terrible finality. A grizzly was chasing and attempting to catch a dodging moose calf while its mother tried to intervene. She rushed the bear repeatedly until it suddenly turned on her. The drama ended with the death of the struggling cow, torn up and pulled down by the bear, while the tourists watched in tears...

During the 1992 North American Symposium on Wolves, held in Edmonton, Alberta, François Messier summed up what was known about moose and predator systems, based on 27 published studies from across North America. To test empirically whether predation can regulate moose numbers, Messier drafted four conceptual models by way of computer simulations. Based on data provided by the field studies, Messier calculated that moose would stabilize at 200 per 100 km^2 in the absence of predators, and at 130 per 100 in the presence of only one predator, the wolf. If moose productivity was further diminished by poor habitat or by bear predation on calves, moose density dropped to 20-40 per 100 km^2.

At an earlier symposium, and based on his own comprehensive studies in Quebec, Messier had warned that, if people were to share the moose with natural predators and if wildlife managers wanted to avoid major prey declines, the hunter's share of a moose population should not be greater than 6 or 7 percent. That was, after all is said and done, the "surplus" that could safely be "harvested." It remains to be seen how such a deal would strike those arguing around the campfire...

Chapter 17

STAND-OFF AT THE CHASM

One of the rare candid-camera films of wolves and caribou is *Following the Tundra Wolf,* much of it shot from an aircraft over the snow-covered barrens of northern Canada. It was not difficult for the crew to locate a herd of caribou since they often rest on frozen lakes, not to soak up the sun as some might think, but as an anti-predator strategy; sleeping animals do not want to be ambushed in the hills. On the ice, they can see their enemy from afar. At the approach of predators, the herd flees only reluctantly, no farther than necessary to stay out of harm's way. The film shows plenty of footage of wolves attacking and chasing the caribou but always without success, until the final episode...

The fleeing herd, a swarm of tiny dots streaming across the screen like a school of fish, caves in when the predator makes his final dash, accelerating in an astonishing burst of speed held in reserve. While the camera zooms in for a tighter focus, the wolf singles out one of the caribou. He pursues the dodging animal, seizes it by one of the hind legs and holds on until a second wolf arrives. It lunges at the struggling prey and brings it down in an explosion of violence. Powerful imagery with a mixed message for the sensitive viewer. However, in a pleasant, reassuring voice, the narrator intones that this is the way of the wolf and the caribou. All is as it should be. It is the way of nature...eternal.

The man behind the sexy voice is Robert Redford. With champions of that caliber is it any wonder that the northland's most prominent predator, formerly reviled as a bloodthirsty varmint, has become the wild variety of "man's best friend" and the beloved symbol of wilderness to masses of city people? During the past two decades or so, the wolf's story has been told and retold in the printed word as well as in paint, film and video. One of the most educational efforts was the traveling exhibit *Wolves and Humans* designed by the Science Museum of Minnesota. Displayed in major cities from Florida to Alaska, from California to Canada, over two-million people saw the multi-media show before it reached its final destination at the International Wolf Center in Ely, Minnesota. Yet, there is a need for more. In the words of the center's co-founder, David Mech: "The public is eager, almost greedy for information about the wolf, for books, television shows, lectures, and even hands-on participation in wolf research."

What has all this sudden celebrity meant for wolves? It has led to a tremendous improvement in status and official protection across North America, to a halt in government sponsored killing, to demands and plans for the reintroduction of the species to regions from where it was exterminated long ago. But also to an increasingly polarized debate between wolf defenders, mostly city-people, and residents of the Canadian and Alaskan backwoods who would like to see a return to limited control so as to enhance wild game stocks. No matter how ancient the issue, how simple the question may seem to some, the two sides have stuck to their guns, perpetuating the endless debate that seems to be leading nowhere, resulting in inertia of government agencies and in covert reaction from some hunters and outfitters whose resentment has been building over years of fruitless dialogue.

How to resolve the dilemma? Although those who oppose wolf control are not necessarily all anti-hunting, by and large, the wolf debate has come down to a matter of hunters versus non-hunters. The chasm between them runs deep. The two extremes adhere to a different set of values regarding living creatures. Shooting wildlife for sport or subsistence is more than just a hobby or profession, it is a way of life. The paradox of hunters is that they kill what they love. In ecstasy, after lining up the telescopic sights of a rifle, he (or she!) terminates the life of the magnificent elk bull strutting among his harem. Just as happily, feeling proud and justified, they may destroy a wolf after chasing it to exhaustion on a snowmobile or in an aircraft. By contrast, to the non-hunter, shooting a wild animal is unthinkable and almost as repugnant as killing a human being.

Is the chasm too wide for reaching across? Surely, a way to the other side can be found! After all, both parties stand on common ground, sharing a deep interest in the natural world. And there is hope in the simple fact that attitudes, even those that have been ingrained over centuries, are not immutable. They can and do change, particularly in this age of instant communication in the "global village." In the not too distant past, it was common practice to destroy hawks and owls, including the now celebrated peregrine falcon, because they competed with humans for small game. The practice is now frowned upon and illegal. Many modern-day hunters are passionate conservationists, actively working for the preservation of nature, including the great predators. Their thinking about wolves has matured. An understanding between hunters and non-hunters, a bridge across the chasm, should not be impossible to attain and is much overdue.

At the 1991 North American Wildlife and Natural Resources Conference, biologist Ralph Archibald, then carnivore manager of British Columbia, described the dilemma to his colleagues in these words: "Wolf control programs have been demonstrated to increase ungulate numbers, but they have created such heated public controversy that there is little political will to support them.... The seemingly obvious solution then would be to abandon these programs, but consider the cost... Our experience shows that, if wildlife managers do not address the concerns of those affected by wolf predation, they will take matters into their own hands, at great cost to wolves and other carnivores."

What does the scientific community have to say about wolf control now, after decades of debate and mountains of evidence? Not much, at least not publicly. Understandably, like other professionals, many biologists have a stifling fear of committing themselves to a view that is not expedient or that may later turn out to be wrong. "The idea that scientists are objective and open to new ideas is folklore. They can become dogmatic, tunnel-visioned and mean, because they cannot transcend their humanity." So said geneticist David Suzuki, host of the internationally acclaimed television series *The Nature of Things*. In a feature about wolves, he lamented that science had been used against wolves "to manage and control them, to tame the spirit of the wild." Ironically, Suzuki, or his script writer, seemed to have fallen into the same trap of subjectivity; the program failed to do justice to, or even to acknowledge, the viewpoint of wildlife managers.

At symposia about wolves, most university and government biologists have remained neutral. Researcher Ludwig Carbyn summed up the quandary: "From a scientific perspective, wolf control to increase ungulates is perfectly acceptable, but it has become socially unacceptable." It takes courage to take a strong stand, either against or in favor of control. At a public forum on wolves that I organized in 1990 on behalf of Canadian Wolf Defenders and attended by an overflow crowd of wolf lovers, hunters, trappers, biologists, politicians and media people, William Fuller, retired dean of zoology at the University of Alberta, admitted: "If we believe in wildlife management, then it seems that there is no reason to exempt any one species." In other words, we manage moose, deer and elk, so why not wolves?

Few are as straightforward as Alberta's carnivore manager John Gunson, who believes that the northwoods could be made into a paradise of big game animals *and* their predators. "We have great wildlife habitat in the north of this province, on productive soils, but we have ended up with low ungulate populations and low predator populations. Northern Alberta could support a great wildlife industry, including both consumptive and non-consumptive components. Aboriginal peoples and other Albertans would benefit tremendously under a regime of large-mammal restoration."

As an example of the kind of productivity that could be sustained on provincial soils, Gunson mentions Elk Island National Park, a fenced oasis of poplar woods not far from Alberta's capital city. It contains an astonishing ungulate density of 1,850 animals per 100 km² (38 miles²), including 350 moose, 1,850 elk, 1,100 bison and 350 deer! Hunting is not allowed but ungulate numbers are culled yearly by wardens to keep them within the limits of their food supply. The park is 195 km² (75 miles²) in size, and there are neither bears nor wolves.

Gunson definitely does not advocate the total removal of all wolves and/or bears from the more remote portions of the province. Management would include temporary reductions followed by restoration. Both factors are part of good management, as pointed out repeatedly by Gunson's colleagues in British Columbia, Alaska and Yukon. Coupled with careful management of hunting and habitat, wolf control would be the key in bringing up game populations, not only for the direct benefit of people, particularly native tribes, but also ultimately for wolves, other predators and scavengers, in short, for the entire ecosystem.

Does it all just boil down to a question of numbers? Can we really expect to manage a highly social animal such as the wolf in the same way as we harvest moose? Or is there an important qualitative aspect that is being overlooked? These fundamental doubts were raised by Gordon Haber, an outspoken critic of past, present and planned wolf control actions in Alaska and British Columbia. Haber is an independent wildlife researcher who has studied wolves and their prey species in Denali National Park for nearly three decades. He injected a note of fresh thinking in the old debate that has struck a chord with wolf defenders everywhere.

"To claim, as most wolf biologists do, that it is okay to harvest up to half of a wolf population just because it will recover to the same size next year, makes about as much sense as claiming that there would be no problem in suddenly trading away half the prime players of a Super Bowl football team because a like number of college rookies will be available to replace them in spring.

"For an animal like this, there is no way we can intelligently, from a biological standpoint, go out and hunt them on any large scale. Other than in the most recent, insignificant eye blink of evolutionary time, the wolf has no substantial history of exploitation by other species. All of its evolution, cultural as well as genetic, is in the opposite direction, producing exceptionally close cooperation by which to exploit other species. If we knock half a population out every year, we may soon end up with the same number of wolves again, because they can breed rapidly, but we basically shred this underlying social fabric which so sets them apart. In this case, numerical status - simple abundance - is not an appropriate criterion by which to determine if everything is okay.

"It just doesn't make biological sense to say that we can harvest an animal like the wolf the same way -let alone much more heavily-than we harvest moose, for example. Moose are near the opposite end of the gradient of sociality, the asocial end. They have somewhat of a social structure, but it is very basic. Hunters can shoot four moose out of a group of ten, and within five minutes the rest will be carrying on pretty much as if nothing ever happened. Species such as moose are already equipped at birth for survival. They're fairly precocious and most of what they need for survival is already genetically there."

In 1985, in recognition of the depth of the chasm between the two sides and to steer the debate to a realistic resolution, I, as spokesman for the Canadian Wolf Defenders, made a bold proposal. Why not divide the country into zones for hunters and non-hunters? After careful consideration and within certain limits, wolf control would be acceptable in some zones, but not in others, and large areas should be set aside where no killing of any wild animals would be permitted. It would give environmentalists a lever to enlarge the number and size of provincial parks with full protection for all species, while professional game managers would be free to show what they could do in hunting reserves. It remained to be seen which zone would ultimately attract the most visitors!

In principle and in practice, zoning is by no means a novel idea. More than a century ago, Yellowstone, the world's first national park, was designated as a no-hunting zone. Likewise, there are already vast regions where hoofed animals are managed by humans only and where large predators were removed long ago. All across North America, there are tremendous wildlife inventories available to hunters on lands devoid of wolves or bears. Since hunters comprise no more than ten or twelve percent of the general population, why do they want proportionately so much, including all of the northern wilds? The reality is that northern residents want to kill an increasing share of native ungulates, for their own use as food or for guiding non-residents. Big game outfitting is an economic, sustainable activity in which northeners want to maximize opportunities with minimal interference from outsiders who do not live in the North.

In 1988, at the Vancouver Wolf Symposium, B.C. carnivore manager Ralph Archibald announced that the provincial government would give the zoning proposal a try. His department would establish a Wolf Working Group, a public advisory board, to work out a system of zones accommodating the various needs of all interested parties: hunters, outfitters, trappers, native people, naturalists and environmentalists. The objective was to get everyone involved in the decision-making process and to maintain a productive dialogue that would eventually lead to an acceptable compromise. The group met several times each year and generated much well-intentioned discussion. Yet, it advanced only as far as the chasm allowed and froze into inflexibility at the same deep split as before. While most parties recognized the need for limited control of wolves on agricultural lands, most non-hunters were unyielding on the question of control to benefit hunters. Tentative proposals to designate some areas as control zones have all been frustrated by intransigence on the part of those who see the zoning idea simply as a cop-out. On wildlands, they want no government control at all, period! In Alaska, the wolf debate ended in the same impasse.

In 1990, following B.C.'s example, the Alaska Department of Fish and Game appointed a Wolf Planning Team, a citizen's advisory committee, to work out a zonal scheme to share the land. Contrary to B.C., where talks went on endlessly, Alaska set a target date for a final report, which came out in June of 1991, after six monthly meetings. The *Strategic Wolf Management Plan* proposed to conserve the state's wolves in six different ways, ranging from full protection to intensive management. Government wolf control by aerial shooting would take place in only two zones.

Very soon after news of the impending kill had been broadcast across the nation, the office of Governor Walter Hickel received an avalanche of irate letters from across the USA, Canada and Europe, running 100 to 1 against control. Several powerful animal rights groups headquartered in California and New York immediately threatened economic blackmail by calling for tourism boycotts. The hard-ball tactics proved instantly effective and resulted in the cancellation of planned conventions at local lodges and hotels. Alaskan tourist operators, who feared that the damage to their industry exceeded the alleged benefit of wolf control to hunters, pressured the state's legislators, who very quickly capitulated and suspended all plans for the year.

Alaskans were outraged. The *Ketchikan Daily News* wrote: "The issue is not wolf control. It's about political power and state's rights. Who controls Alaska, state residents or congress and national environmental organizations?" The *Peninsula Clarion* thought that "the decision to cancel wolf control was an example of emotions overwhelming common sense."

In the hope of finding a compromise solution, the Governor invited 120 representatives from across the spectrum of interest groups to a Wolf Summit, where experts went over the facts, figures, opinions and proposals one more time. In his address to participants, Walter Hickel said that he was open to all ideas except one: "I will not be part of the state of Alaska giving away its sovereignty over management of fish and game. I believe in wolf management."

But after all was said and done, the Summit changed little or nothing, and all plans for wolf reduction by the Alaska Fish and Game Department were cancelled. In an editorial, the *Anchorage Daily News* declared: "The American people will not tolerate state-sponsored aerial wolf hunting. Period. Angry Alaskans can parade, posture and pout until the Yukon River dries up, but the outcome will be the same... Aerial wolf hunting is a nasty, bloody business and no amount of antiseptic talk about "management" will hide the truth. Aerial wolf hunting's day has passed, and it's foolish to pretend that some compromise can be worked out to satisfy sportsmen, the tourism industry, environmentalists and animal rights activists."

In January 1993, during the darkest days of the Alaskan winter, the chasm looked deeper and wider than ever before....

Chapter 18

IN THE FINAL ANALYSIS

Alaska sprawls over more than half a million square miles. There are twice as many caribou as people and for every two citizens there is one moose. More than enough big game, it seems, for those who hunt for sport or subsistence, considering that they comprise about a quarter of the state's population. So why the perennial complaints about low moose numbers, and why the recurring demands for wolf control? To explain their view that moose densities are in fact very low, and as an illustration of what could be achieved by predator reduction, some wildlife managers point to Sweden, a northern country less than a third the size of Alaska. In a good year, Swedes fill their freezers with 150,000 moose, as many as the entire population estimate for the northern state, where the 1993 harvest totalled a mere 7,000! Why the immense difference? Firstly, hunting in Sweden is strictly regulated. Secondly, there are no winter ticks, allowing great densities without the risk of fatal infestations that are inherent to North America. And thirdly, there are very, very few large predators in Scandinavia. The "norra norland" is haunted by the odd bear and the number of wolf packs can be counted on the fingers of one hand. Yet, as ridiculous as it may seem, even there, in the most wildlife-loving society on earth, the last of mankind's wild competitors still raises howls of protest from some hunters. In fact, perhaps unique in the world, Sweden has an organisation dedicated to the destruction of the wolf. A few years ago, the corpse of a yearling was ritually mutilated in an infantile exhibition of ancient hatred and prejudice.

By comparison, Alaskans have shown great tolerance and even pride in the fact that the state contains the largest population of wolves in the USA. Estimated in 1993 at 5,900-7,200, their continued abundance is in no way threatened, particularly now that the days of government wolf control seem to have come to an end. Yet, the depth of feeling against wolves held by many northerners and the cultural imperative to kill them can never be underestimated. The emotions that separate advocates of control and those who feel that wolves should be left alone defy consensus and leave wildlife managers stumbling in an ethical minefield where biology and economics provide no guidance. Field biologists can provide stacks of objective data to clarify the issues, but ultimately the resolution of the age-old wolf debate depends on values that are beyond the reach of science.

Faced with the prospect that any large-scale control of predators would be paralysed by persistent public protest, what are governments going to do about their ongoing desire to reduce wolf predation on at least part of the game range? Alaskans have been in the forefront to explore several non-lethal methods. Diversionary feeding is based on the premise that a predator with a full belly should have no need to hunt for the young of ungulates. To test the practical merits of this idea, the wildlife department dumped carcasses of train-killed moose in areas where predation on calves by bears and wolves was perceived as a serious problem. The moose carcasses had been stockpiled during winter and were transported to the test site by helicopter during May and June. Initially, the consumption of this carrion, mainly by bears, indeed led to better calf survival, but the cost of the program was very high and it was eventually abandoned as not viable.

Other methods to reduce predation on moose were to let alternate prey species, such as caribou, become more numerous so that they would take the brunt of wolf and bear attack. Moose numbers could further be raised by prescribed burning of mature woods creating young growth which favored browsers but not bears. Perhaps the most promising, albeit hazardous idea in the quest for an effective, socially acceptable form of wolf control was to artificially reduce the birth rate. Various categories have been tried on dogs and captive wolves, such as steroid hormones, analogs of pituitary and hypothalamic hormones, immuno-contraceptives, chemical sterilization and chemical castration. Based on her research, Cheryl Asa of the St.Louis Zoo came to the following conclusion: "Sterilization is all we are left with. All other possible methods have side effects. However, if we were to be successful in preventing the production of offspring in wild canids, what would the consequences be for the social system of the wolves? If the alpha female would not become pregnant, would she eventually leave to find another male? And what would be the possible long-term social effect on the pack from the failure to produce young?"

Professional wildlife managers such as David Kelleyhouse, Alaska's director of wildlife conservation, hoped that "reproductive physiologists in the lower 48 will eventually develop a birth control technique which can be effective under field conditions." In the meantime, he proposed to place a greater reliance on conventional methods of ground-based wolf control such as trapping and hunting, which has also been the way government departments have compromised on the issue in much of Canada.

Both British Columbia and Alberta have actively encouraged the taking of wolves by private citizens. Open seasons are long. Registered trappers are given traps or snares and are invited to attend workshops for instruction in the most effective techniques.

In Alberta, some trappers are even provided with baits in the form of carcasses of road-killed hoofed mammals. Dumped year-round at designated sites, the meat attracts wolves which become used to the free lunch, until the tragic day when all access to the baits is blocked by snares and traps.

Such specialization by private wolf getters can be very deadly and is called "hidden control" by those who oppose government involvement of any kind. In some form or other, hidden control takes place furtively and unobtrusively in all regions where there are wolves. The methods used are not only trapping, but also hunting with snowmobiles and aircraft, especially in the far north. In Alaska, the preferred hobby of private wolfers is to fly over the wilderness and locate their hapless target from the air. Termed "land and shoot hunting" or "aerial trapping" the practice is regulated and licensed by government, but the extent of illegal actively is difficult to measure in the vastness of the North. Some Alaskan pilots could be tempted to operate across the border in Canada where law enforcement agents are very thinly spread. As rumor has it, frustrated by lack of action from government, unscrupulous Canadian outfitters are doing some local wolf control on their own, by dumping poison baits from aircraft over their remote holdings, virtually free from the risk of discovery and prosecution.

What, in the final analysis, is the state of wolfish affairs across North America today? In the lower 48, the animal is protected under federal legislation as an endangered species and cannot be legally hunted, at least not yet. However, at over 2,500 strong now, population estimates for Minnesota are increasing to the point where wildlife managers foresee a need for the reopening of a trapping season. More and more loners and pairs are spilling over into neighboring Michigan and Wisconsin. In the northwestern states, wolves are also expanding and now number several hundred in Montana, Idaho and Wyoming. Wolf recovery may eventually include the Dakotas as well as the southwest and southeast if current plans for reintroduction come to fruition.

In Canada, the total wolf estimate for 1993 was in the neighborhood of 56,000. Quebec, Ontario and British Columbia each have around 8,000; the prairie provinces about 4,000 each; the Northwest Territories and Yukon together close to 15,000. As reported by wildlife departments in all of these jurisdictions, wolves are maintaining themselves or expanding their range everywhere. Considering the heated publicity that has poisoned the atmosphere for so long in the northwest, how do other Canadian provinces cope with their substantial inventories of what is, after all, a very controversial predator?

While Alaska, British Columbia and Yukon have been embroiled in bitter disputes for years, Ontario, Quebec, Manitoba and Saskatchewan have quietly avoided the limelight, apparently managing their wolves in a way that is acceptable to its citizens. Problem wolves in agricultural zones are removed by government agents. On wildlands, wolves are subject to conventional trapping and hunting but not to government predator control, even though complaints about wolf numbers are routinely received from local hunting groups.

When we look at the state of affairs as objectively as we can, it cannot be denied that there is a *de facto* system of zoning in place from Quebec to British Columbia. In all provinces, there are four different zones: (1) total absence of wolves in settled regions; (2) heavily exploited populations in marginal agricultural lands; (3) natural wolf populations subject to trapping and opportunistic hunting in unoccupied wildlands; and (4) designated pockets of full protection in parks and preserves.

Over time, as human development continues to expand, both zones 1 and 2 are bound to grow in size. In zone 3, as well as 2, it stands to reason that wolf and ungulate densities vary greatly, depending on habitat quality and proximity to roads, waterways and native communities. In Alberta, perennial complaints about low moose numbers are received from the northern portion of the province. Yet, there are pockets of abundance not far from the capital city of Edmonton and in the Peace country on the edges of agricultural lands where bears and wolves are kept low by trappers, hunters and government predator officers.

Zone 4, perhaps the most important from the perspective of naturalists and wolf lovers, includes areas of full and complete protection where trapping and hunting of predators *and* their prey species is not allowed. Pockets of such ideal designation are numerous, including most national and provincial parks. However, the crucial question is: are these sanctuaries large enough to contain a wide ranging carnivore such as the wolf? The reality is that none of the existing parks that offer full protection within their boundaries is, in fact, large enough. For instance, a third of the population of Algonquin Provincial Park is killed by trappers each winter when the wolves follow deer herds outside the park. In Banff and Jasper National Parks, nearly all wolf territories straddle the boundaries. The province of British Columbia does not contain *any* large parks, either national or provincial, that fall into category 4, where trapping and hunting are not allowed.

Demands for the enlargements of parks with full protection should be a bargaining tool in all government proposals to control wolves elsewhere. Parks and preserves that have proven too small should be enhanced by the addition of adjacent areas or by the enforcement of a buffer zone of protection around the park. Along the same vein, Monte Hummel, the energetic president of World Wildlife Fund Canada, has been negotiating since 1991 with provincial and territorial governments for the creation of so-called Large Carnivore Preserves that include or surround core areas of full protection such as the parks.

A fascinating story to watch is the return of the wolf to the world's oldest national park, Yellowstone, which contains a very high density of prey species. Somewhat smaller than Jasper, it has thirty times as many elk! Inside Yellowstone's boundaries the herds are neither culled by hunters nor by park rangers, who maintain that the grazers are regulated by food supply. Each winter, several thousand elk starve to death! Now that the reintroduction of wolves into the park has become a howling success, there is no doubt that *Canis lupus*, the former outlaw, wily and adaptable, will regain more of his rightful place in the American West and elsewhere.

As pressures on our wildlands increase and as the human population continues to expand, a productive and realistic accommodation between hunters and non-hunters, between livestock owners and wolf lovers, is long overdue. The common denominator among these various interest groups should be that the wolf has intrinsic value of its own. This book was written to further that goal, to find common ground between people who take a passionate interest in the evolving wolf story.

Chapter 19

JASPER TODAY AND TOMORROW

Park wardens get many questions from wildlife-loving tourists. The one they hear most often is about wolves: "How many are there?" It is also a key question for park managers charged with the preservation of the priceless inventory of this magnificent national treasure. But the answer, in the enigmatic lyrics of folk singer Bob Dylan, "is blowin' in the wind."

Of course, there are official estimates although the exact figure is elusive and ever-changing. What is a park wolf anyway? To qualify for that status, does it have to belong to a pack denning inside Jasper's boundaries? Or could it be any individual of this footloose species that spends some time of the year, or part of its life, inside the park? Which ever formula we choose, a reasonably accurate head count would require a continuous and costly field survey.

For better or worse, wildlife in Canadian National Parks has been researched little compared to parks in the United States, such as Yellowstone, Denali or Isle Royale. Jasper's wolf population has never been subjected to the kind of intensive monitoring possible today with technical gadgets. In parks where a dozen or more animals run about with radio-collars around their necks, it is possible to distinguish one pack from the other and to arrive at a reliable total. Yellowstone's wolves, after their release in 1995 and 1996 were all equipped with at least a conventional transmitter, if not with the most up-to-date satellite or capture collars. The latter contain anaesthetic needles that can be triggered by remote control, making it possible to recapture the animal if the batteries need replacing or if the animal strays too far outside the park and turns its predatory eye to livestock.

Besides keeping track of the Yellowstone population, the researchers continue to amass many fascinating details of the wolves' habits. In two or three years, they had already witnessed more direct interaction between wolves and elk than observers in Jasper over fifty years. But radio-telemetry carries a hefty price tag.

In 1992, the cost of a radio-collar that beams its signal to an orbiting satellite was around $4,000, plus a similar amount for one year of data-processing, if the collar lasts that long...! Some fail after a few weeks or months, others are lost by the animal's premature death. The cost of a three-year program in Alaska, using satellite equipment, was calculated at about $30,000 per pack. This was supposed to be good value; conventional collars that are cheaper to purchase require monitoring by fixed-wing aircraft or helicopters that rent at five or six hundred dollars per hour!

Field use of radio-collars on wolves was pioneered by David Mech in the Superior National Forest of Minnesota in 1968. At that time, little was known about wolf movements. The first collared wolf that dispersed from its place of birth travelled 210 km (130 miles) in a straight line! Since then, the quickly accelerating use of telemetry has led to mountains of data and new understanding of wolf population dynamics. Recent technical innovations have spawned a new catch phrase called "landscape ecology" involving so-called Geographic Information Systems, which allow researchers to superimpose animal travel routes onto a colorful screen showing the topography and habitat.

In Jasper, over the years, there have been two wolf studies that included the limited use of radio-telemetry. In 1983-1985, the Alberta Fish and Wildlife Division monitored the Brazeau pack from the air, producing an excellent series of data on predation rates. The study also showed that these wolves, which denned inside the park, ranged as far as 55 km (33 miles) away onto provincial lands.

In 1989-1992, several collared wolves belonging to packs denning in the lower Athabasca valley were followed, mostly on foot, by biologists Ward Hughson and John Weaver. They reported that the animals routinely crossed park boundaries, which was well-known before the age of telemetry, but now verified and undeniable, a point that might prove useful in future negotiations with trappers and provincial wildlife managers. Both studies indicated high mortality rates on the boundaries. One of the instrumented wolves was trapped at Rock Lake. After a long struggle, probably lasting several days, the wire that secured the trap to a tree broke and the animal limped back into the park, dragging the leg-hold and chain. It was subsequently darted from a helicopter and let go again after removal of the trap. In this case, the fact that it was collared turned out to be a life saver!

While biologists are having great fun satisfying their curiosity about this once elusive predator, not everyone is convinced that there is a need for such detailed research in a national park. To some people it is sufficient to know that the wolves are out there, wild and free, part of the mystique of wilderness. Others object in principle to the radio-collaring of park animals since it constitutes harassment, starting with their capture in leg-holds and snares, or pursuit in helicopters and shooting with tranquillizer darts. No matter how well-intentioned and careful, all methods are heavy-handed and include a small risk of accidental injury or death. To be caught in a paralysing trap and handled by a human adds up to a traumatic experience for a wild wolf, probably increasing its shyness. If the trapped wolf is an alpha female, she may lead her pups and the pack away from a long-used site as soon as people come close. She might have tolerated the intrusion before but now has learned to associate people with danger. Since the choice of dens and rendezvous sites by Jasper wolves is very traditional, their forced move has consequences for the large mammal system of the surrounding area. In the same way, relentless snow-tracking of collared animals during late winter can be a form of harassment, especially if the animals are disturbed near a traditional whelping den. For this reason, conscientious researchers back-track their animals.

While short-term monitoring of pack movements always leads to some interesting vignettes of wolf ecology, over the long term it is of limited value and may even result in a misleading picture of pack territories and travel routes which are by no means cast in stone but subject to frequent change at the whims of the wolves themselves or through the interplay of a host of other factors.

Over the years, the tendency in Jasper Park has been to monitor its wolves through a hands-off approach, by opportunistic sightings over the long term. Observations are reported and entered into a computerized data bank. The main contributors are wardens and naturalists, some of whom spend a lot of time in the backcountry. Others drive the roads on a daily basis. Much of Jasper's terrain is semi-open, making it possible to see more than a glimpse of the wolves, especially during winter when they often travel by day. Year-round wolf habitat in the park is restricted to the major valley systems which are patrolled by wardens. For that reason alone, their reports should form a good basis for estimating the park's total population. In fact, all such figures given by government biologists who have studied Jasper's wolves during the past fifty years were based on warden sightings, as well as their own.

However, there is no denying that sightings can lead to false conclusions. For instance, three reports of respectively 4, 8 and 5 animals, seen in the lower Athabasca district over a period of several weeks, do not add up to a total of 17 wolves. Packs commonly separate and come together again. All we can say is that the minimum number was eight, unless we can be certain that there were different groups involved. This is possible by noting the wolves' color; if one pack includes only black animals and the other grays, the possibility of duplication can be dismissed. The wide variation in pelage makes for striking differences between wolves; some blacks have a gray body or whitish feet, others a silvery face, neck and tail. Gray animals can be quite plain or variegated with dark accents, and the tail can have a more or less prominent black tip. The sum of details makes it possible, for the astute observer, to recognize individual animals, which is a helpful key in distinguishing one pack from the other.

The next question often asked by tourists is: "Where is the best place to see wolves?" Here again, the answer is blowin' in the wind. A traveling wolf may show up anywhere, along roads as well as in the backcountry. The best chances are in open terrain along the major rivers. Wolves occur in the alpine uplands too, particularly during summer and fall, but denning packs generally stay in the valleys that thaw out earliest.

All major river systems have wolves: Smoky, Snake Indian, Moosehorn, Athabasca, Rocky, Brazeau, Whirlpool and Miette. The fact that these drainages are separated by mountain ranges makes it likely that each contains a discrete group. Since packs usually include six to ten members, the total number of wolves in the park should be a minimum of 48 and a maximum of 80, give or take a few loners, and assuming that all valleys harbour a denning pack each and every year, which may not be the case. Of course, during late summer the population swells by the addition of pups, but dispersal and attrition may soon bring it down again to roughly what it was before.

As described in Chapter 6, a major fluctuation occurred in Jasper's wolf population during the 1970s and the official estimate increased to 80-100. The real number may well have been much greater. During those years, when prey numbers were high, there were three denning packs in the Snake Indian drainage alone, and large groups of 18-25 animals were reported from the Smoky, Moosehorn, Miette and Brazeau districts. By 1983, wolf estimates dropped steeply to 27-40. In the meantime, it has climbed to 40-50 and remained near that level as far as is known.

A characteristic of wolf population dynamics everywhere is that packs can build up quickly in formerly vacant territory. All it takes is a meeting of two loners of the opposite sex resulting in one brood of healthy puppies. Come autumn, a pack of eight or nine emerges from the woods where none had been known to occur before. By the same token, long-established dynasties may suddenly vanish if pups and/or adults fall victim to disease, starvation or human-caused calamities. In 1983, a traditional denning area near Willow Creek became deserted following the rumored shooting of five adult wolves on the park's north boundary. During the same year, the well-established Devona pack disappeared for unknown reasons. It is suspected that it may have been knocked out, perhaps on a poison bait, across the boundary at Brule Lake where there is a grazing lease for cattle and horses. Fortunately, the following winter, a pair re-established itself at Devona and brought pack membership back up to nine by October.

The vulnerability of Jasper's wolves points to the need for special status in neighboring provinces, British Columbia to the west, and Alberta to the east. The grazing lease between Bedson Ridge and Brule Lake at the lower end of the Athabasca valley is in a critical spot, right on a major travel corridor for park wolves. Since only one rancher is involved, it would seem quite simple to cancel the lease and return the area to game range. It would also be wonderful if an arrangement could be made with provincial trappers guaranteeing a buffer zone of added protection. This is particularly important where boundary lines seem to have been drawn rather arbitrarily, right across a valley. An example are the muskegs and open hill sides at Rock Lake that form a natural route into the Willow Creek district of Jasper. An agreement between the park and the government of Alberta, enhancing protection in this vital corner seems long overdue and easily accomplished since it would affect only one registered trap-line and very few hunters.

Perhaps even more serious than their vulnerability on adjacent provincial lands, is the fact that Jasper's wolves suffer a high mortality *inside* the borders. These wilderness travellers are not street-smart and have been reported to collide with cars and locomotives they could see and hear coming from afar. Known wolf mortalities on Jasper's roads and railways from 1980 to 1990 amount to 23, for an average of two or three annually. This number appears to be increasing. Ten wolves, including eight pups, were killed in 1996. In the narrow Bow River corridor of Banff Park, traffic fatalities have led to concern for the viability of the valley's wolf population.

Another species which frequently runs afoul of vehicles and trains is elk. Locally it represent a check on herd size, slowing the trend to overpopulation, which may not be a bad thing. However, the machines kill indiscriminately, across all age groups, whereas natural predators are selective in the culling of prey species. Unfortunately, while elk are concentrating near human habitation, wolves hesitate to follow. Far ranging as they are, they run afoul of hunters on the boundaries and do not easily lose their innate fear of people especially during pup-raising time. Although, there are some notable exceptions....

During June of 1993, a pack of three frequented the edges of the townsite and the Whistlers campground, where they were known to have killed at least five elk calves. The wolves were often observed at close range by wardens and tourists and seemed to have become habituated to the presence of people. Their lack of shyness was probably due to their feeding at sites where park staff had been dumping the carcasses of traffic-killed elk over the previous winter. The wolves did not seem to have stayed for very long after elk calving time and were not seen in the same area the following spring. In the past, during the 1940s, wolves occupied dens not far from the townsite at Buffalo Prairie and probably along the Overlander Trail. There has not been a known case of successful breeding in these prey-rich montane habitats for some time, though it is quite possible that some cases may have escaped attention in the rugged environs. In 1995 and again in 1996, a large pack of twelve or thirteen raised its pups not far from the Snaring campground. This proves that some wolves, if unmolested, are not too shy to follow their prey close to well-traveled roads.

In contrast to elk and wolves, other ungulates are generally less affected by the presence of people in the park. White-tails and mule deer are common in the townsite but also everywhere else. Moose, mountain goats and caribou do not search out human-use areas. They are loners or live in small groups, spread thinly over vast regions in order to avoid detection by predators.

Bighorn sheep are in a category by themselves. They congregate on winter ranges at lower elevations, but find safety from wolf attack on rocky cliffs. Sharp-eyed and wary, they can take care of themselves and do not seek the company of people. However, locally, where the highway borders on steep terrain, some bands spend more and more time along the road during winter. Attracted by de-icing chemicals, they lick the pavement oblivious of traffic that passes by within meters. The problem is aggravated if the sheep refuse to go back up to alpine heights in spring, which is their ancestral way of avoiding predators and a build-up of harmful organisms. Year-round residence on the same range carries an increased risk of contagious disease or parasites, as well as increased problems with traffic.

By and large, the unnatural concentration of ungulates along roads has led to serious repercussions for the park's large mammal system, as well as to the increasing risk of collisions. Moreover, after elk discovered that people are harmless, even defenceless, close encounters between elk mothers and unwary tourists have led to injury. The fact that visitors are charmed by the presence of "tame" elk on lawns and golf courses should not make us complacent and accept the situation as inevitable. It is the paradox of the park that its precious inventory of wildlife, its wolves and its elk, need our protection, but they do not need us.

How to resolve the dilemma? Park planners have recommended that the townsite be made less attractive to grazing animals by recreating a more natural ground cover instead of lawns. School grounds and public greens should be fenced. A drastic resolution would be to fence off the entire townsite and to put Texas gates on access roads. There are precedents in other countries. In African parks, tourists and campers are restricted to closed compounds for their own protection. In Banff, sections of highway have been fenced to prevent collisions and the animals are supposed to cross the roads via underpasses. Where possible the highway should go underground so that animals can pass over the traffic tunnel on natural ground along traditional game trails. Another possibility for areas of critical importance is to raise sections of road on stilts, allowing wildlife to pass underneath.

Unless efficient measures are incorporated, the ecological integrity of the park will be further jeopardized as traffic and visitors continue to increase year after year. With tourist dollars up for grabs, the insidious rot of development will spread from within. Park managers face a seemingly hopeless battle to hold back the creative forces of those who wouldn't think twice about turning the place into Disneyland North. Yet, consideration for park values has begun to spread among all parties, including the business community. Thirty years ago, the Jasper Chamber of Commerce was clamoring for roads across the Skyline Trail and up the Snake Indian Valley, all the way to Rock Lake and beyond to the remote solitudes of Azure Lake and the Ancient Wall. In this day and age, when the conservation message has spread, such schemes appear utterly impossible, or so I hope.

The gravest concern centers on the Athabasca valley, the heart of the park, where both predators and prey are deeply affected by the growing presence of people. How Jasper, this jewel-in-the-crown of Canadian National Parks, will cope with its problems in the future remains an interesting sequel to watch. As the twenty-first century approaches, will wolves continue to hunt the age-old valley, to manage the elk and sheep as nature intended? Or will they be squeezed out? It is an important question to ask. And the answer is once more blowin' in the wind, the winds of change - change that is inevitable. May most of it be for the better, to the benefit of wildlife and humans alike!

Chapter 20

TALES OF A WOLF WATCHER

A tiny pup tent set on a fragrant bed of conifer twigs can make a seasoned back country hiker feel quite at home in the bush, if the location is well-sheltered. The dense branches of a big spruce serve as a natural umbrella that provides shade from the sun and a refuge from rain. Sitting against the trunk and with the warm glow of a good fire at one's feet, even the bleakest days may be endured in relative comfort. Traveling as light as possible, usually solitary, I selected my camp sites on the edge of a meadow, not too far from a wolf rendezvous site.

My greatest worry was bears, especially when fresh tracks and scats were in evidence. At night, when the wolves barked in alarm, I suspected that they had unwelcome visitors, a black bear or grizzly, and I lay awake for a long time, startled by every small noise. In the morning, when daylight returned and I had obviously made it safely through another night, my courage returned. Near camp there was usually a tree that could be climbed as an escape route in case of an emergency. In my early years I was so anxious that I checked the tree by actually climbing up some distance and removing dead branches that were in the way, until a sliver of bark fell into my eye, causing discomfort that lasted the rest of the trip. I realized then that my greatest enemy was undue worry.

Over the past decades, the popularity of hiking has increased tremendously and anyone who now travels Jasper's backcountry has to obtain a permit, subject to a strict quota or reservation system. One has to provide details of the route and pay in advance for each overnighting. Hikers are also required to camp on certain sites, where metal boxes are provided for those who want to light a fire. In the most popular sites, after years of use, the ground becomes worn and the trees end up shorn of their lower branches so that they provide little shelter from wind and rain. In the mountains, where the temperature on a wet summer day can dip close to freezing, a drafty and muddy camp site is a depressing place to be. Moreover, food scraps left by careless people attract bears that become increasingly bold. Generally, they do not bother sleeping people unless there is food inside the tent. However, there have been a few incidents in which grizzlies ripped the canvas and pulled campers out of their sleeping bags, apparently for no reason at all.

Despite my worries about bears, I continue to give in to the lure of the wild. In daylight the threat seems less acute, especially when one is in the company of others. One of the basic rules about safety in bear country is to announce one's approach by making noise, especially while traversing a dense belt of trees. But I got tired of talking to myself or hitting trees and rocks with a stick. Often I fall silent, so as not to ruin the tranquil atmosphere of the day. Walking noiselessly on mossy ground or wet grass is enjoyable in itself. Relaxed but supremely alert and on edge, I sometimes spot a bear before it sees me. The discovery is always startling. If the animal becomes aware of me and moves away, my courage or foolhardiness returns quickly. If it stands its ground, perhaps because there are cubs nearby, I slowly back off. To be honest, at the end of each trip, when I have once more made it safely back to the road, I feel a sense of relief.

The question of whether or not to run away and climb a tree when one sees a grizzly has been debated time and time again, in books and articles, and among my travel companions. At the start of a trip, we usually remind each other to stand our ground if challenged. Running might trigger a bear's predatory instinct and many a fleeing person has been overtaken. Standing still in the face of danger is the best defense. But that is easier said than done, as we found out when the moment of truth arrived. We had discovered the grizzly from a safe distance, through the binoculars, and we watched it for half an hour. Accompanied by a pair of yearlings the sow was digging for the roots of peavine on a partly wooded island of the Snake Indian River. Eventually, the trio departed, the two cubs following their mother in single file. We hadn't had our breakfast yet and returned to camp, elated about our observation. An hour or so later, we decided to head over to the island to look for signs of the bears' activity.

After fording the shallow river channel, we separated along the shore of the island. My companion stayed in the open on the gravel bars and I followed a set of wolf tracks up a game trail that led through a small grove of poplar trees to a narrow ditch, a former river channel. Here, several huge bear prints were clearly imprinted on the mud. I shouted to my friend to come over for a look. At the sound of my voice an unseen animal started running in the woods. Elk, I assumed, since we had observed several the day before. Again I shouted to alert my friend, hoping that he would be able to see the elk leave the island. Instead, it was a grizzly! It came straight at me, parting the bushes like a locomotive. "A bear!" I screamed, "Don't run!" The grizzly halted and rose on its hind legs, looking gigantic. My buddy's running footsteps were loud on the gravel. I couldn't control myself either and ran back a few paces down the trail. Off to one side was a big poplar and I thought of climbing it. But I could hear the bear jump down the bank and come after me. I stopped and froze, facing the trail, binoculars slipping out of my hand....

The bear approached, hesitated, snorted, then continued down the trail. The next moment, it splashed heavily through the river. It was followed by a pair of large yearlings. Each of them came to a full stop at arm's length and turned to face me. Then they too bounded on, splashing through the water. My friend, standing some distance away on the river bank, had a clear view of them, but I had been unable to focus. "Your face was as gray as your beard!" my buddy said afterwards.

Only quite recently has it become possible to purchase a new kind of "equalizer" that gives hikers a chance to repel aggressive bears. This long-awaited defensive weapon is the pepper spray can. Light-weight and easy to handle, it carries a potent irritant that can turn the biggest brute around, if you hit it right in the eye or on the nose. The instructions may state that its range is up to nine meters (30 feet), but that seems an exaggeration, especially if the wind deflects the spray. If you aim against the wind, you may even knock yourself out! I for one have never tested it on bears, but I did on myself, accidentally.

It is with a certain relief that the wolf watcher welcomes winter. When the weather turns cold and snowy, bears retire into an underground shelter to sleep until spring. Or so we assume. In Jasper, the backcountry hiker is well-advised to carry the spray well into November. To prevent the propellant from freezing, it has to be kept in one's pocket, which can be risky unless the safety catch is secure. I had lost mine and taped a wood chip under the trigger. One cold morning, this improvised security system failed while I sat down on a log. The can fired in my pocket! After an attempt at washing the sprayed areas of pants and underwear, my hands became thoroughly contaminated and felt as if I had spilled boiling water on them. Whenever I touched my eyes, nose or lips, they began to sting. The bears must have been laughing....

Anyway, for the wolf watcher, winter is the best of seasons with many advantages over summer apart from the absence of bears: no stifling heat, no rain, and no biting insects. After the leaves drop, chances of seeing the wolves improve. They travel far and wide, often on frozen lakes and rivers. Moreover, in snow, we can find clear evidence of their presence. Following tracks leads to discovery; we learn interesting details about the habits of these mobile predators, as well as about the lie of the land. We get to see places we would otherwise never visit.

To reach my study area, I frequently make a short-cut by crossing the Athabasca River. After several weeks of very cold weather, the ice is solid. However, channels of water may open up at any time as the current wears away the ice from below. One day a companion and I were following the tracks of a pack of eight that crossed the river, which was covered with a fresh fall of snow. The animals were well spaced out, but near the middle they all met at one spot where they proceeded in single file. It alerted us to our peril. Testing the ice with a stout pole, we found that there was a channel where the ice was dangerously thin. The pole plunged through even on the spot where the animals had made it across. We could just imagine how one of the older wolves had led the way and called the younger members of the pack to heel.

When crossing frozen rivers, one should use the greatest care, even to the point of being over-cautious. I always carry a long pole and often employ improvised skis: sturdy "two-by-fours" fitted with a simple leather strap that holds the boot in place. Some of my companions have scorned this awkward and heavy equipment, but in situations that are potentially life-threatening, brawn is not a good substitute for brain. Those who are the most fearful should lead, not the bravest. Humans can take a clue from other social creatures that have been around for much longer than our own species. The elk herd is guided by an "old woman" not by the mighty stag. Bands of bighorns, that inhabit treacherous, steep country, follow an experienced ewe.

Crossing the Athabasca River during fall or late winter, when the water was open or packed with ice floes, could be equally perilous. At first we used a canoe but replaced it with an inflatable raft that was very much lighter to carry. However, dinghies can spring a leak. I experienced some panicky moments when one of the two airtight compartments blew. My boat instantly became a floppy bathtub that was very hard to handle and full of cold water. Fortunately, I was able to reach the shore.

During winter, our shelter for the night was a tent of the kind often used by hunters or native people. Made of heavy canvas, it was about three by four meters (10x12 feet) in size and high enough in the center so that a person could stand up. The ridge pole and its A-frame supports at either end consisted of slender but sturdy pine trunks that we had cut in the woods nearby. The tent had no floor. Before setting it up, we had to select a level spot, scrape away the snow and remove stumps and sticks. Inside we made ourselves comfortable with seats and beds improvised from boards and blocks of wood. Our pride of place was a small, light-weight sheet-metal stove, its rusty pipe going up through a hole in the roof, protected with a patch of fire-proof material. This little stove could do miracles with a few tinder-dry twigs and branches. In a matter of minutes the cold interior of the tent was transformed into a toasty warm environment that allowed us to take off jackets and sweaters. Wet socks, mitts and boots were hung up to dry. The air-tight stove is surely one of the greatest inventions of mankind, second only to the wheel. On the coldest of days, the temperature inside was tropical. When darkness fell, the back of the stove and the lower end of the pipe glowed red. Seen from outside, the black forest all around, our home looked like a glowing womb, illuminated by the golden light of candles.

After we went to sleep, the unattended fire ran out of fuel quickly and the cold reclaimed our abode. On some nights the thermometer fell to -36° celsius (-35°F)! Tucking our head into the sleeping bag, we were quite comfortable, most of the time, while frost collected on the inside of the canvas. Getting up at first light, it took only a handful of twigs and a match to get the stove going again and once the ice had melted, the pot of water boiled in minutes.

We passed the day wandering far and near, using snowshoes if needed, exploring a variety of special places: a tree-studded marsh with a series of beaver ponds; a spectacular canyon where cougars stalked across the rimrock; a spring-fed creek that stayed open all winter and where schools of small trout stood in the weedy current. We learned where an otter might leave its tracks, where foxes staked out their territory, and where a few moose were clipping the willows. We counted the deer and classified the herds of elk and sheep. And, over the years, we kept track of the wolves. Seeing them or finding fresh sign were the highlights of a trip. Among the many smaller pleasures of every day was to return to a well-organized camp and rekindle the life-sustaining fire for a meal or hot drink.

Near the end of March, we carried the tent and stove out, strapped to our pack frame, to be stored for another season, until we were forced to change our ways. In the early 1980s new winter camping regulations came into effect, restricting where and when one could set up a tent and make a fire. However, to support the continuation of my wildlife observations in the area, park authorities permitted the use of a small patrol cabin. The sturdy, well-constructed log hut had been there for decades, largely forgotten and bypassed by the wardens who patrolled the district by truck or snowmobile. A narrow track that was closed to the public ran past the cabin, leading to the rail siding some distance farther. The road was frequently traveled by service vehicles, but after deep snow drifts blocked access the cabin became isolated. That was the time I liked it best and I went there every two or three weeks.

Mishaps are most worrisome when one is alone, particularly if illness strikes. One December evening, while a north wind was whining through the spruces, I developed a severe case of stomach cramps. All night I was sick as a dog. The morning dawned dark and depressing with a full-scale blizzard blowing. That day I was scheduled to return home. Perhaps it would have been better to stay until the situation improved. However, I had no way of contacting the outside world. In desperation, I decided to make a run for the road, about 3 km (2 miles) away. The snow was gusting horizontally over the meadows, but after I entered the woods, as if by divine intervention, a pale sun came out. With rising spirits I walked along briskly in the lee of the trees and reached the river in less than half an hour. The current was choked with ice floes, the dinghy partly deflated and buried in snow drifts. I dug it out and pumped up the air pressure. Then I exchanged my big felt packs for rubber boots and carried the gear and the raft to the water's edge. Launching the dinghy when an open lead appeared in between the massed floes, I reached the opposite shore in minutes.

The car was parked in its usual spot, covered in snow. The starter turned over briskly but the engine would not fire; it had been too cold the previous night. Planning to hail a passing motorist, I was hooking up a tow chain, when the snow plow stopped: "Seen any wolves?"

The guy obviously had heard what I was doing here in this frigid no-man's-land. But at times like these, wolves are low on my list of priorities. I had not seen any, besides there were more urgent things on my mind. Would he please be so kind as to pull me up a ways? A little later, the old engine came to life and I was on my way home. The long four hour drive to the big city is wearying and violates all my pedestrian sensibilities. Turning on the radio hits like culture shock. Yet, the irritation is mellowed by gratitude that another trip to the wilds has had a happy ending, the hardships all but forgotten. And soon I want to go back again... and again.

References

Ballantyne, E.E. 1955. Rabies control programme in Alberta. Canadian Journal of Comparative Medicine 20:21-30.

Bailey, B., M. Sloan, and J. Lidle. 1993. Wolf! Special Alaska Issue. 11(1):13-32.

Bailey, B., M. Sloan, and J. Lidle. 1993. An interview with David G. Kelleyhouse. Wolf! 11(2):9-14

Bergerud, A.T., W. Wyett, and B. Snyder. 1983. The role of wolf predation in limiting a moose population. Journal of Wildlife Management 47:977-988.

Burpee, L.J. (Ed.). 1907. The Journal of Anthony Hendry, 1754-55 - York Factory to Blackfeet Country. Royal Society of Canada. Pages 307-354.

Carbyn, L.N. 1975. Wolf predation and behavioral interactions with elk and other ungulates in an area of high prey diversity. Ph.D. Thesis. University of Toronto.

Carbyn, L.N. 1989. Coyote attacks on children in western North America. Wildlife Society Bulletin 17:444-446.

Cowan, I. M. 1947. The timber wolf in the Rocky Mountain National Parks of Canada. Canadian Journal of Research 25:139-174.

Cowan, D. 1986. The strange death at Suffle Lake. Outdoor Canada, summer issue 1986:14-17.

Dekker, D. 1985. Wild Hunters. Canadian Wolf Defenders Publication.

Dekker, D. 1986. Coyote preys on two bighorn lambs in Jasper National Park, Alberta. Canadian Field-Naturalist 100:272-273.

Dekker, D. 1986. Wolf numbers and color phases in Jasper National Park, Alberta: 1965-1984. Canadian-Field Naturalist 100:550-553.

Dekker, D. 1987. The not-so-natural history of Jasper National Park.

Park News 23(4):26-29.

Dekker, D. 1988. The wolf debate: control or no control - The Vancouver wolf symposium, May 10-11, 1988. WolfNews 6(2):1-6.

Dekker, D. 1989. Population fluctuations and spatial relationships among wolves, coyotes and red foxes in Jasper National Park, Alberta. Canadian Field-Naturalist 103:261-264.

Dekker, D. 1990. David Suzuki: What governments do to wolves on our behalf. WolfNews 8(3):5.

Dekker, D. 1990. Interview with B.C. carnivore specialist, Ralph Archibald. WolfNews 8(1):2-3.

Dekker, D. 1990. Public Forum on wolf management in Alberta - Lots of applause, a few boos and lots of laughter. WolfNews 8(1):4-6.

Dekker, D. 1991. Managing wolf/prey populations - The scientists' viewpoint. WolfNews 9(2):2-3.

Dekker, D. 1991. Lament of a wolf manager. WolfNews 9(2):2-3.

Dekker, D. 1991. Interview with Alberta carnivore manager John Gunson. WolfNews 9(1):3-4.

Dekker, D. 1992. Second North American symposium on wolves - Their status, biology and management. Edmonton, Alberta, August 25-27, 1992. WolfNews 10(3):1-8.

Dekker, D., W. Bradford, and J. Gunson. 1995. Elk and wolves in Jasper National Park, Alberta - From historical times to 1992. Pages 85-94 in: Ecology and conservation of wolves in a changing world. (Eds. L.N. Carbyn, S.H. Fritts, D.R. Seip). Canadian Circumpolar Institute, Pub. No. 35.

Edmonds, E.J. 1986. Restoration plan for woodland caribou in Alberta. Alberta Forestry, Lands and Wildlife.

Errington, P.L. 1967. Of Predation and Life. Iowa State University Press.

Farnell, R., and R.D. Hayes. 1991. A

case history of intensive management: Yukon's Finlayson caribou herd. Yukon Fish and Wildlife Branch Report.

Fritts, S.H., W.J. Paul, L.D. Mech, and D.P. Scott. 1992. Trends and management of wolf-livestock conflicts in Minnesota. U.S. Fish and Wildlife Service Resource Publication No. 181.

Fuller, T.K. 1990. Dynamics of a declining white-tailed deer population in north-central Minnesota. Wildlife Society Monograph 110.

Gasaway, W.C., R.O. Stephenson, J.L. Davis, P.E.K. Shepherd, and O.E. Burris.1983. Interrelationships of wolves, prey and man in interior Alaska. Wildlife Society Monograph No. 84.

Glover, R. (Ed) 1962. David Thompson's Narrative, 1784-1812. The Champlain Society, Toronto.

Godwin, L. 1990. Woodland caribou in northwestern Ontario - Why they are different. Ministry of Natural Resources Technical Notes No. TN-07.

Gunson, J.R. 1963. Wolf predation on livestock in western Canada. In: Wolves in Canada and Alaska. L.N. Carbyn (Ed.) Pages 102-105.

Gunson, J.R. 1991. Management plan for wolves in Alberta. Alberta Fish and Wildlife Division Report.

Gunson, J.R. 1992. Historical and present management of wolves in Alberta. Wildlife Society Bulletin 20:330-339.

Haber, G. 1992. Wolf-moose systems, suspension bridges and apple trees. WolfNews 10(2):2-4. (Abridged from an interview in "Wolves and Related Canids" spring issue, 1992. Ed. Debbie Warrick.)

Hayes, R.D., and D. Mossop. 1987. Interactions of wolves and brown bears at a wolf den in the northern Yukon. Canadian Field-Naturalist 101:603-604.

Hayes, R.D., A.M. Baer, and D.G. Larsen. 1991. Population dynamics and prey relationships of an exploited and recovering wolf population in the southern Yukon. Yukon Fish and Wildlife Branch Report.

Horejsi, B.L., G.E. Hornbeck, and R.M. Raine. 1984. Wolves kill female black bear in Alberta. Canadian Field-Naturalist 98:368-369.

Hummel, M. 1990. A conservation strategy for large carnivores in Canada. World Wildlife Fund Canada.

Hunter, R. and P. Watson. 1986. Cry Wolf! Shepherds of the Earth Publications, Vancouver.

Leopold, A. 1966. A Sand County Almanac. Oxford University Press, New York. Mech, L.D. 1966. The wolves of Isle Royale. Fauna of the National Parks of the U.S.A. Series No. 7.

Mech, L.D. 1967. The Wolf. The Natural History Press, New York.

Mech, L.D. and M. Korb. 1978. An unusually long pursuit of a deer by a wolf. Journal of Mammalogy 59:860-861.

Mech, L.D. 1984. Predators and predation. Chapter 8 in: White-tailed Deer, Ecology and Management. L.K. Halls (Ed.). Stackpole Books.

Mech, L.D. 1990. Who's afraid of the big, bad wolf? Audubon 92(2):82-85.

Messier, F., and M. Crete. 1985. Moose-wolf dynamics and the natural regulation of moose populations. Oecologia (Berlin) 65:503-512.

Messier, F. 1985. Solitary living and extraterritorial movements of wolves in relation to social status and prey abundance. Canadian Journal of Zoology 63:239-245.

Messier, F., C. Barrete, and J. Huot. 1986. Coyote predation on a white-tailed deer population in southern Quebec. Canadian Journal of Zoology 64:1134-1136.

Munthe, K., and J.H. Hutchison. 1978. A wolf-human encounter on Ellesmere Island, Canada. Journal of

Mammalogy 59:876-878.

Murie, A. 1944. The wolves of Mount McKinley. U.S. Department of the Interior Fauna Series No. 5.

Peterson, R.O. 1977. Wolf ecology and prey relationships on Isle Royale. National Park Service Scientific Monograph Series No. 11.

Peterson, R.O. 1984-1993. Ecological studies of wolves on Isle Royale. Annual reports.

Pimlott, D.H. 1961. Wolf control in Canada. Canadian Audubon 23:145-152.

Pimlott, D.H. 1967. Wolves and man in North America. Defenders of Wildlife News, Study 5:36-47.

Potvin, F. 1988. Wolf movements and population dynamics in Papineau-Labelle reserve, Ouebec. Canadian Journal of Zoology 66:1266-1273.

Potvin, F., H. Jolicoeur, and J. Huot. 1988. Wolf diet and prey selectivity during two periods for deer in Quebec: decline versus expansion. Canadian Journal of Zoology 66:1274-1279.

Rutter, R.J. and D.H. Pimlott. 1968. The World of the Wolf. Lippincott Company, Philadelphia and New York.

Schmidt, K.P. and J.R. Gunson. 1985. Evaluation of wolf-ungulate predation near Nordegg, Alberta. Alberta Fish and Wildlife Division Report.

Scott, P.A., C.V. Bentley, and J.J. Warren. 1985. Aggressive behavior by wolves toward humans. Journal of Mammalogy 66:807-809.

Seip, D.R. 1990. Wolf predation, wolf control and the management of ungulate populations. In: Wildlife 2001. D.R. McCullough and R.H. Barrett (Ed.). Elsevier Applied Science, London and New York. Pages 331-340.

Seip, D.R. 1992. Factors limiting woodland caribou populations and their interrelationships with wolves and moose in southeastern British Columbia. Canadian Journal of Zoology 70:1494-1503.

Singer, F.J. 1990. The ungulate prey for wolves in Yellowstone National Park. In: Wolves for Yellowstone? Volume II: Research and analysis. A Report to the U.S. Congress. Pages 2:3-37.

Stelfox, J.G. 1969. Wolves in Alberta: a history 1800-1969. Alberta Lands, Forests and Wildlife Magazine 12(4):18-27.

Stelfox, J.G. 1971. Bighorn sheep in the Canadian Rockies: a history 1800-1970. Canadian Field-Naturalist 85:101-122.

Strickland, D. 1988. Wolf howling in Algonquin Provincial Park. Algonquin Technical Bulletin No. 3.

Suzuki, D. 1991. The dark side of science: mean, jealous and dogmatic. Environment Column, Edmonton Journal 3-10-1991.

Theberge, J.B. and D.A. Gauthier. 1985. Models of wolf-ungulate relationships: When is wolf control justified? Wildlife Society Bulletin No. 13: 449-458.

Tompa, F.S. 1963. Problem wolf management in British Columbia: conflict and program evaluation. In: Wolves in Canada and Alaska. L.N. Carbyn (Ed.). Pages 112-119.

Warrick, D. (Ed.). 1992. Wildlife scientist interview: Dr. Gordon Haber - Views on wildlife management. In: Wolves and Related Canids 5(1):16-21.

White, P.A. and D.K. Boyd. 1989. A cougar kitten killed and eaten by gray wolves in Glacier National Park, Montana. Canadian Field-Naturalist 103:408-409.

Young, S.P. 1970. The Last of the Loners. The MacMillan Company, New York.

Young, S.P. and E.A. Goldman. 1964. The Wolves of North America. Dover Publications Ltd, New York.

Index

206

For up-to-date information on wolves and management issues, contact the following organizations:

International Wolf Center,
Publishers of *International Wolf* Magazine,
1396 Highway 169,
Ely, MN
55731-8129 USA
Phone 1-800-ELY-WOLF
Wolf Web Site http://www.wolf.org

Wolf Park,
Publishers of *Wolf!* Magazine,
Battle Ground, IN
47920 USA
Phone 317-567-2265
E-mail wolf@dcwi.com

Canadian Nature Federation,
Publishers of *Nature Canada* Magazine,
Suite 520 - 1 Nicholas Street,
Ottawa, Ontario
Canada K1N 7B7
Phone 1-800-267-4088
E-mail cnf@web.net

World Wildlife Fund Canada,
90 Eglinton Avenue East, Suite 504,
Toronto, Ontario,
Canada M4P 2Z7